Simple
&
Profound

Other books by David du Plessis

A MAN CALLED MR. PENTECOST
THE SPIRIT BADE ME GO

Simple & Profound

DAVID du PLESSIS

PARACLETE PRESS

ORLEANS, MASSACHUSETTS

© 1986 by Paraclete Press
Library of Congress #: 85-63854
ISBN #: 0-941478-51-3
All rights reserved.
Published by Paraclete Press
Orleans, Massachusetts
Printed in the United States of America

TABLE OF CONTENTS

FOREWORD

Just before my young editor friend and I began work on this book, I found myself trying to remember the answers that I had given to some of the difficult questions which Christians face, as they get serious about walking with the Lord. I tried to remember the things that sounded really good to me, when I said to them, and then write them down.

But it didn't work, no matter how hard I tried. Finally, I said, "Lord, help me. I can't remember that answer. Why is my memory so bad?"

Why do you want to remember it?

"I would love to use it again."

You might use it, when it isn't suitable.

I had no answer for that.

Remember where you got it.

"I got that answer from the Holy Spirit."

Then, when you need it again, He will give it to you again. Do not try to capitalize on what you learned from the Holy Spirit. Remember: you cannot use the Holy Spirit. He will use you.

That, of course, corrected my whole attitude. I don't have any gifts that I can use, but the Giver of all the gifts has got me, and He uses me and gives the right gift at the right time to the right people. And that is what this book is all about: simple answers, simple stories — but not so simple, when you think about them.

Why am I putting them in a book now? It seemed about time, and they were the sort of thing that I've been sharing in public for most of my more than eighty years — ever since I met Sam Shoemaker in Pittsburgh. I told him a whole lot of things that he asked me about, and he looked at me in a funny way and said: "You know what you are? You are a spiritual miser."

"A miser?"

"Yup, you've got a wealth of experience, wonderful things to tell. Why don't you tell it?"

"They'd think I was bragging."

"Well, you must brag on Jesus, of course."

"You think I should?"

"Look: Jesus told stories. We call them parables. Some of His parables most likely were incidents that happened. You don't have to tell parables; just tell your stories of what happened, what you learned, and so on. And remember: never preach on a text that you haven't experienced, and never tell an experience without a text to validate it."

It was pretty good advice, and I've tried to stick to it, ever since.

David du Plessis
Pasadena, California

1

THE HOLY SPIRIT

For more than half a century, the author has been considered a world authority on the nature and work of the Holy Spirit, so it seemed appropriate to begin this book here. But before we speak of the Holy Spirit, we must begin at the beginning.

How does a sinner get saved?

By the shortest prayer that Jesus ever prayed: "Father, forgive them; they know not what they do." That is unconditional forgiveness. He shed His blood in that moment, and that is the cleansing flow, the blood that makes the difference between saints and sinners. How do you become a saint? By the cleansing blood. His blood cleanses us from all unrighteousness.

First, you must acknowledge to Him that you are a sinner and need to be forgiven. Then you ask — and accept — His forgiveness, and the cleansing of His blood, which washes away all sin. Next you invite Him into your heart, to abide there, the rest of your days. And you turn your life over to Him entirely, no strings attached, accepting Him as your Lord, as well as your Saviour.

Once you are His, you are eligible for the baptism in the Holy Spirit, and that can follow immediately, although that is not usually the case. In the house of Cornelius, when Peter preached and spoke of remission of sin, that household accepted the remission of sin, and the moment they did, they were baptized in the Holy Spirit. They were not circumcised, they were not baptized in water, but they were candidates for the baptism in the Holy Spirit, because they'd been cleansed from sin. There you find the drink of living water and the baptism on top of it in the same meeting.

Incidentally, we call that the Gentile Pentecost, because we read that until then they had preached the Gospel to Jews only, for ten years. And when he returned to Jerusalem, Peter was in trouble with the Church's elders. "You ate with these uncircumcised!" they reprimanded him, "You actually *ate* with them!"

"But I have done nothing," he testified. "I didn't lay hands on them. I didn't do anything. I didn't even pray for them. In fact, I was preaching forgiveness, when the Lord baptized them in the Spirit."

How do you feel about altar calls?

I changed my mind about altar calls at the end of meetings, when I began to receive letters from people who had received the Baptism, while listening to my tapes. So I prayed one day, "Lord why are the tapes so successful, and I often don't see similar results in the meetings?"

The answer I seemed to hear was: *In the meeting, because of the custom of an altar call, they all wait for you to pray for them at the end, but listening to the tape, they know that no one will be praying for anyone. So they begin to surrender, or begin to understand that the Lord is talking to them.*

I came to the conclusion that the altar call is just a tradition, and it can actually do a lot of harm. Too many people go forward, believing that they have not received anything, while the preacher was preaching; they have been just waiting for the prayers afterwards.

No longer do I give them the chance to just wait. At the end, I say to them: "There's no altar call, but I've got three challenges for you: salvation, healing, and the Baptism. Now, how many of you tonight want salvation? You have heard me, and you have believed what I said, but you have not confessed that you have accepted what I said. Now will you say, 'Yes, Lord, I'll pray for salvation?' By saying, 'Yes, Lord,' that means that you have not only heard the blessing and the promise, but you've accepted it." And this works miracles.

Are any Christians ineligible for the Baptism?

When brethren ask me, "How can you now go out and invite these infant preachers who are not baptized properly, to come and accept the baptism in the Holy Spirit?" I reply: "Jesus proved to me that He baptized the family that had not been circumcised and had not been baptized. They were forgiven, born again in a moment, and baptized there. But they were not children; they were adults. Jesus will never baptize a child, because the baptism is for ministry, and a child cannot minister."

A Lutheran disagreed: "I got all that when I was a baby."

"When?"

"When they baptized me. I got all that when I was a baby. I got water baptism, salvation, baptism in the Holy Spirit, everything."

I looked at him carefully. "You don't look like someone who has all that. You look very miserable to me."

Another man standing there, turned to him and said, "I want to tell my brother here that I also tried to believe what he is now saying. I had been ordained for twelve years, when I found that I wasn't born again, and I wasn't baptized in the Holy Spirit. And I was getting nowhere. But now that the Lord has saved me and baptized me in the Holy Spirit, my church is flourishing."

So, just as your baptism in water is not something that is there and then disappears, and then is there again, the Baptism in the Holy Spirit is permanent. It is one anointing, and you remain under that anointing. Jesus said, "The Spirit of the Lord is upon me, He *has* anointed me." He did not say, "He is anointing me."

Why do some call Him "Jesus," while to others He is "Christ"?

After a meeting in New England, a minister came up to me and said, "How can you so easily say Jesus, Jesus, Jesus all the time?"

"Well," I replied, "I know Him personally. You know, it's just like my friends — when I first meet them, and they don't know me personally, they call me Mr. du Plessis, or Dr. du Plessis, and so on. But after they get to know me, they just call me David." I paused and looked at him. "And you can't say Jesus?"

"No."

"Then you haven't met Him yet. You need an experience. You know about Him, but you haven't *met* Him."

He came back for the meeting the next night and the next, and while I don't know what all the Lord did for him, later he did invite me to speak at his church. There, talking with him at lunch, I noticed that he was saying Jesus all the time.

"Glory to God!" I interrupted, "you've had a great change!"

"How do you know?"

"You can say Jesus now." I find today in the Charismatic Movement that there is less speaking of Him as the Christ, and so on. They know Him and they love Him, and they just call Him Jesus. Wherever I go to speak, I always say to people I have come to talk about Jesus. And the Scripture does not say that Christ is the head of the Church; Jesus is the Head of the Church. It's the man, Jesus. He is the Anointed One, true. But why speak of the anointing, as if that were all? It *is* the anointing upon Jesus, and that anointing is what makes us Christians, yes, true. But the Head of the Body we belong to is Jesus.

What do you mean by "the experience of the Holy Spirit"?

Understanding the experience of the Holy Spirit is very simple, if you take notice of what Jesus did, and how He spoke about the Spirit. A theologian came to Him — not to ask, as the little hymn put it, 'the way of salvation and light' — but to discern the source of His manifestation of power. "You must be a man of God, but how do you do these miracles?"

Instead of answering directly, Jesus said: "If you are not born again, you cannot see the Kingdom of Heaven." What does that mean? It only means you're blind. A blind person isn't dangerous; he just needs a little help.

"But how can you be born again?" the man persisted, and look how simple Jesus makes it: by water. Now what is water for? When you hear of water, do you think of washing your face? Or do you think of a swim? No! Where does water begin for anybody? It is a *drink!* The reason why John 3:5 is so controversial is because the Baptists have tried to make the water mentioned there, water baptism, and others have interpreted it as natural childbirth. I say it is the Holy Spirit.

The Spirit is water?

In the 4th chapter of John, when Jesus speaks to the woman at the well, He refers to the Spirit as "living water."

"But," a theologian once said to me, "after Pentecost, that changed."

"Then you haven't read to the end of the Bible yet," I replied. "Because I read in Revelation: 'I am the Alpha and Omega, the beginning and the end. I will give to him that is athirst of the fountain of the water of life freely. And he that overcometh his thirst shall inherit all things, for I will be his God, and he will be my son.' That's the new birth! And the new birth doesn't stop. It's still there; in fact, this water and drink business is the last message to the Church, before the trumpet sounds, and Jesus comes. In the last chapter of Revelation, it says: 'The Spirit and the Bride say: come, let him that heareth say come, and let him that is athirst, take the water of life freely.' That is salvation, the new birth! Without this drink, you cannot see the Kingdom, you are not in the Kingdom, but if you have had your drink of Water, you are born of the Spirit, you are full of the Spirit, and you have got a well in you that will keep bubbling up into everlasting life! That is what He said. The drink is what prepares you for the future; for heaven."

He also said, "If you believe in me, as the Scripture says, out of your belly will pour rivers of living water." This He spoke of the Spirit, which the disciples had not yet received, because Jesus had not yet been glorified.

"Full of the Spirit"
— is that the same as "Spirit-filled"?

"Spirit-filled" is a common expression in the Pentecostal Movement, based on Acts 2:4 — "They were filled, and they spoke in tongues." But I have had to abandon that Pentecostal traditional teaching, for to me it is absolutely false. I have never seen any baptism yet — immersion, pouring, or sprinkling, that gets one drop in. It is *on* them, not *in* them. I have never heard a priest or any minister say, "Now, mother, open up his mouth, and let me give him a sip." Nothing gets into you by baptism, and you are certainly not filled by baptism. You are filled by a drink.

Jesus said: "If any man thirsts, let him come to me, and drink." He did not say: "He will be baptized." He spoke only of drinking. And he said: "And if you believe in me, as the Scripture says, out of your belly (not after the baptism, after the drink) you'll have rivers of living water pour out of you." This He spoke of the Spirit, which they had not yet received.

But what did Paul mean by "be filled with the spirit"?

"Be ye not drunk with wine, wherein is excess, but be filled with the Spirit." (Eph. 5:18) It is a good word, but it does not mean *get* filled; it means *remain* filled. It means pouring over, because the moment he says be filled with the Spirit, he follows it with: "speaking to yourselves in psalms and hymns and spiritual songs, singing and making melody in your heart to the Lord, giving thanks always for all things unto God, and the Father in the name of the Lord Jesus Christ, submitting yourselves one to another in the fear of God." That's a long sentence, and a lot of doing. But it is what you *can* do, if you are overflowing with the Spirit.

In Acts 2:4, it says: "and they were all filled with the Spirit." Remember, *upon* them was fire; they were baptized in fire and saw the tongues of fire. But *in* them was water, because Jesus had breathed on them and said, "Receive ye the Spirit." Notice, He did not talk of baptism; that was when He met the ten disciples. (Only ten? Only ten, because according to the law, no synagogue could be established with more or less than ten. Ten was the perfect example; they could not commence a synagogue meeting, until there were ten men on the floor.) And Jesus did something wonderful: He breathed on ten men, and said, "Receive ye the Spirit." And, "As my Father sends me, so send I you."

And what is the next word? *Forgive.* "Whosoever you forgive are forgiven." The first assignment of the ten men who were born of the Spirit was to forgive. (If only the Church had gone on and remembered that, at its birth, ten men received the Spirit and were given the assignment to forgive everybody!) If you don't forgive, we are taught, you are not forgiven — "Forgive us, *as* we forgive those that trespass against us."

"Filled with the Holy Ghost, they began to speak in other tongues as the Spirit gave utterance" (Acts 2:4). The "filled" here had nothing to do with the fire that was on them; it meant that they started speaking. And that you can trace from the beginning of the Gospels — Elizabeth, filled with the Spirit, spoke. Zacharias, filled with the Spirit, spoke. Every time there is "filled with the Spirit," there's speech, speech, speech. Peter, in difficulty, standing before the Sanhedrin, was filled with the Spirit, and said: "Ye rulers of the people and elders of Israel" — every time you get the word "filled," it is followed by speech, and that means overflowing.

In Acts 4:31, we read: "And when they had prayed, the place was shaken, where they were assembled together, and they were all filled with the Holy Ghost, and they spake the word of God with boldness." That "filled" does not mean this was a re-baptism. This was another overflowing, "out of your belly will flow rivers of living water."

Are tongues, then, the initial evidence of being filled with the Spirit?

People say: "You must speak in tongues, and then you've got the evidence." But I say that while it is evidence of the Baptism in the Holy Spirit, the evidence of being Spirit-filled is love. I now not only refuse to call tongues the initial evidence, I call it the *consequence*, and after that I say: this is the anointing. It is not a filling; it is an anointing.

That phrase "Spirit-filled" is terribly abused today; the correct word that Jesus coined was "anointed" — Spirit-anointed. If you speak of Spirit-anointed, then it is the Baptism. If you speak of Spirit-filled, that is the drink of Living Water — the in-filling. If John had held his converts under water for them to take a drink, he would have drowned them.

Do you have to be Spirit-filled to have the Fruit of the Spirit?

People point to well-known, non-Pentecostal ministers and ask me: "How can many of these men do so wonderfully in their ministry without speaking in tongues or without claiming the Baptism in the Holy Spirit?"

I tell them: "They *are* Spirit-filled, ever since they got their drink, and that produced the fruit of the Spirit. But I must admit, some people do better with their fruit in the Spirit, than others do with the gifts, because the latter have neglected the fruit."

Remember this: you are going to have fresh fruit. Don't try to have dried fruit; you will look like prunes. It is wonderful how Jesus, full of the Spirit, for, shall we say, 18 years, from his 12th year, lived a Spirit-filled life. Then came the Baptism in the Holy Spirit, and He is the Way. He lived a Spirit-filled life and was favored of God and men because of His life. But then, when He got the Baptism, His trouble started.

What happens when a pastor receives the Baptism?

Nothing unseemly, if he has sufficient maturity. But the anointing of the Holy Spirit is a powerful substance — like dynamite. And while dynamite is just the thing for evangelizing the world, in the Church, it is leaven that is needed, not blasting powder. You blow up a church, and you cannot get the pieces back together.

I once knew a young pastor of a large Baptist church. When he came into the Baptism, some well-meaning Charismatic friends, young in the Spirit themselves, urged him on. "Now you've got the power; give it to them with both barrels!"

"So," he told me, "I went into the pulpit, and I blasted them with both barrels. The first barrel blew them out, and the second blew me out, and now I have nothing."

I shook my head. "Your charismatic friends have no understanding of pastoral responsibility. A pastor is a shepherd; he doesn't beat his sheep; he leads them." I put my arm around his shoulder. "Well, you now have only one option: be a doormat. Let them walk on you. Ask them to forgive you for your foolishness. And leave it in the Lord's hands. Whatever happens, you will be the wiser for the experience."

2

OF TONGUES AND INTERPRETATION

Perhaps nothing in the Pentecostal Movement is as controversial as the whole question of speaking in tongues. Here, as elsewhere, the author sheds badly needed light, with consummate simplicity.

What happened to you, when you first spoke in tongues?

The unfortunate thing for me was, I had to unlearn so much of what I had learned in the beginning. When at fourteen, I finally faced the challenge and began to study what the Word had to say on the Baptism in the Holy Spirit, I had the strange feeling that what was going on in our church I had seen before. Only it was not like the Day of Pentecost; it was more like Samaria. Everybody wanted to lay hands on people — I don't know who they thought they were helping, the Baptizer or the candidate. But I thought they were an interfering nuisance.

So, when our church had this conference in 1918, at which they started praying for people to receive the Baptism, I refused to let anyone lay hands on me. I thought: I'll talk to Jesus about it. He saved me out in the country, not in a meeting, and now He must baptize me. I went off by myself and knelt alone in a corner, away from the rest, and asked the Lord to help me, and to baptize me.

I felt something — it seemed like something down inside of me was bubbling up and wanted to come out. I couldn't understand it with my head, but in my heart I began to realize that, while the Spirit was in me already, He had never been *released*. A warm glow now spread over me, and I started laughing. I was overjoyed: Jesus was there, and He was going to baptize me. "Lord," I gasped, "this is strange; I thought the laughter would come afterwards." And that made me laugh all the harder. I started to shout, "Hallelujah!" But the first syllable was all that came out, after that it streamed off into a language I'd never heard before.

There was an old Irish sailor there named Bob Masser, who had been around the world many times, and now he shouted, "Folks, David is speaking pure Chinese!"

That shook me; we had been taught that the Lord gave you the language of the people with whom you would be called to work. Indeed, in the first years of the Pentecostal movement, some of our would-be missionaries even went to foreign lands without studying the language beforehand, so confident were they that the Lord would give them the gift of the appropriate tongue. Those were some of the silly things in the beginning of Pentecost.

"O Lord, don't send me to China!" I begged and stopped praying in tongues. But whatever was bubbling was still bubbling, and I started speaking again. It was a different tongue, and now I felt badly. The Holy Spirit had given me the gift of Chinese; had I grieved Him by my ingratitude? I stopped speaking again, and started again; it was different again. From then on, there was no holding on to just one language; every time I stopped and re-started, it was entirely different. And yet at no time did I feel any compulsion; it flowed out easily.

But now the business of having so many different tongues began to trouble me, and so I went over to a gifted English Bible teacher named Charles Heatley, who had given me wise counsel in the past. "Brother Heatley, does the Lord give you one language for a gift, or more? Because I seem to have been given at least five — is that in order?"

"Indeed it is!" he smiled, opening his Bible and quoting: "to another, diverse kinds of gifts of tongues."

"Oh, I see — that means different languages?" And he nodded. "Well, how many?"

He chuckled. "I Corinthians 13 speaks of the tongues of men and of angels — how many languages are there in the world?"

"Um, I read somewhere that there were around two thousand."

"Well," he laughed, "when you've spoken two thousand, then you can start worrying about the tongues of angels."

That satisfied me, but now the story got around that, because I spoke several languages, I had received the gift of tongues; the others had just gotten the evidence. And now they started saying, "You've got the gift; use it or lose it!" So I used it, at every meeting I broke forth — until I read in Scripture that he that speaketh in tongues in a meeting should pray, that he may interpret.

Duely convicted, I prayed, "I have not interpreted, and I've disturbed the meeting. Lord, give me interpretation." Then I realized that those things which had been coming into my mind, as I spoke in tongues were just that: the interpretation. And here I had discounted them, thinking that it was just my mind, my intellect, jealous for center stage and wanting to be recognized! I had deliberately sought to quench my intellect. But that is the wonderful thing about tongues: you are not in a trance. You know exactly what you are doing; you only don't know what you are saying.

So the next time I felt led to pray aloud in tongues, I took courage and then spoke out what was coming to my mind. I began to praise the Lord for His grace, for His wonderful works. And oh, did that bless the meeting! After that, I realized that I could pray in tongues any time — or all the time, if I wished. In fact, I was often aware that I was speaking in tongues down below, even as something else was going on consciously. With an inner ear, I could hear myself praying in tongues.

What is the most important aspect of speaking in tongues?

Love — always walk in love . . . speaking in tongues is a blessing, but if, as Paul cautions in I Corinthians 13, it is not done in love, it is just noise. "Though I speak with the tongues of men and of angels and have not charity (here 'charity' means love in action; love is a good feeling, but charity is putting that feeling to work), I am merely a sounding brass and a tinkling cymbal." Now that always puzzled me. I never really knew what the

Apostle meant, until one day I called my wife Anna, which I do at night after meetings, to tell her what happened during the day, and to learn what the mail brings.

On this day, I needed her to get some information from my files, so I called during the day, and there was no answer. As I sat there, listening to the phone ring in our empty apartment, I sighed and said, "That telephone can be such a blessing — if you get an answer. But if there's no answer, all you get is a bell ringing." And the Lord said to me: *Now you know what a tinkling cymbal is. It is a ringing without any answer.*

I have been guilty of praying in tongues, praying in the Spirit, and getting no answer. I never knew why, until I discovered that you may speak the tongues of men and of angels, but if you have no love, you're just talking; it doesn't mean a thing. Unless you pray in tongues out of love for the Lord and to have a loving conversation with your heavenly Father, it's just a selfish prayer for yourself. You will not get an answer, and if you don't get an answer, it does not edify.

Does one always receive a recognizable language?

You may not recognize it, and perhaps even a philologist would be stumped, but don't make the mistake of regarding it as gibberish — that's what the enemy would have you believe. I was speaking one evening in Washington about tongues, and afterwards up came this well-dressed lady, highly educated and holding a responsible position in government. "Oh, this has been so encouraging!" she exclaimed, and then she sighed.

"But I have not gotten to the point, where I have a language. I pray in the Spirit, and all I get is a clicking."

"Clicking?" I asked, "What do you mean clicking?"

She was embarrassed. "Well, it sounds like a typewriter. There's no sound, really, just a little variation."

As she was telling me this, into my mind came a recollection of a visit I had once paid to a Pentecostal farmer, in the heart of the jungle of Southwest Africa (now called Namibia). "Sister," I said to her, "if I tried to imitate that clicking, do you think you could recognize it?"

"I think so."

I did, and she clapped her hands. "Yes! That's it, exactly!" And she joined in.

Listening to her, I burst out laughing, and hurt by my reaction, she stopped. "No, no!" I assured her. "It's not you I'm laughing at. But as you clicked, I could see a tribe of bushmen, all under four feet tall, looking at me and clicking away at one another." I stopped laughing. "You see, you *are* speaking a language — the tongue of a tribe of bushmen in Southwest Africa. I met them once years ago, and that is exactly what they sound like."

I shook my head. "Talk about the Lord's mysterious ways — here I am, first time in America, and here you are, a cultured lady with a prayer language from the jungle of my home country."

There is an interesting postscript: shortly after when I visited Darien, Connecticut, I told that story, and afterwards another well-dressed, well-spoken lady came up to me and said, "I'm so glad you told that story about the bushmen's tongue. Because that's my prayer language, too, and I've always been ashamed of it."

When one speaks in tongues, to whom is one speaking?

I believe that speaking in tongues is speaking to God, because the Apostle says: "He that speaks in a tongue, speaks not to men." Why some people always want to speak in tongues in public, I don't know. He that speaks in a tongue edifies himself.

Before you arrive at church, you spend some time in front of the mirror, edifying your face and your dress — why don't we edify ourselves spiritually at home, before we come to church? Why do we want to come and speak in tongues in church in the meeting, where it could be a disturbance?

What is tongues?

Tongues, first and foremost, is prayer. "He that speaks in a tongue, speaks not to men, but to God, for no man understandeth it. Howbeit, in the Spirit, he speaketh mysteries." One old professor said to me, "David, can you tell me what these mysteries are?"

"Yes, I think so, because here I read 'Speaking to yourselves in psalms and hymns and spiritual songs, singing and making melody in your heart to the Lord.' Those are some of the mysteries that you speak — this is the way we praise the Lord."

"Well," he smiled, "I never thought of that."

"Tongues is not nonsense," I concluded emphatically. "It is not just talking; it is speaking to God. And the beauty of it is, the Lord can speak to us."

Tongues is also a gift, but not speaking in tongues; speaking in tongues is a manifestation of the Spirit in prayer. The speaker does not have the gift; the Spirit has the speaker. And what the speaker gives is a gift to the Church.

On the day of Pentecost, when they spoke in tongues, no translation was necessary, because those who heard, understood. It was not speaking the languages of those people; they were not addressing those people at all. They were addressing God. And what did the listeners hear? They heard them speak the wonderful works of God — they were praising the Lord — and the listeners knew, then, that this was a divine manifestation.

Is tongues the evidence of the Baptism in the Holy Spirit?

I was once teaching on the Baptism in the Holy Spirit, and afterwards, as people came up and thanked me, the Archbishop of Canterbury, Michael Ramsey, asked me: "You spoke about the baptism and confronted us with Christ as the Baptizer, but you never mentioned tongues."

I said, "Why should I? Tongues is only the consequence of the Baptism; I don't call it the evidence."

"Yes, but you have not told us whether it's important."

"Who says it is not?"

"Why, all theologians agree that it's the least of all the gifts."

"Oh, yes," I smiled, "I agree with that a hundred percent: it is the least of all the gifts. Which is exactly why you always begin with it and then edify the church with the others."

The people around us laughed, and he could see he had just put his foot in it.

I went on, "Peter, James and John, Mary and all the rest — they all began with it; why don't you want to begin with it? Why do you want the other gifts to happen, when this, the least of all, you won't accept?"

How do you deal with academic experts on "glossalalia"?

In Vancouver, I was invited by a chaplain of the University of British Columbia (the only Pentecostal chaplain on campus) to speak at a lunch-hour meeting there. The meeting had been well-announced and was crowded, and just as we were about to begin, in comes a distinguished-looking gentleman with a goatee. A girl student next to me, clutched my arm. "You see that man coming in there?" I nodded. "That's a Jewish professor, and he's a terror, a real sadist who will make a fool of anybody. He's brilliant, and he destroyed Derek Prince, when he was here. Whatever you do, don't talk to him!"

Inwardly I wished she hadn't told me that, just as I was about to speak — not that I was in any way intimidated, for I love a challenge — but, as it turned out, he went and sat down behind a pillar, and I actually forgot about him. I went ahead and spoke about tongues, and when I closed, and the meeting was over, he started to come down front. My student friends, standing behind me, tugged my coat and whispered, "Don't talk to him!"

The professor came up and said, "I appreciate what I learned from you today, and I wonder: would you be willing to speak to my class?"

"When?"

"Next period — in ten minutes."

"About what?"

"About glossalalia."

"What has your class got to do with glossalalia?"

"We're talking about communication."

"I see. All right, I'll be there."

Startled at this unexpected turn of events, the students around me asked the professor, "Can we come, too?"

He nodded. "Yes, but take the top seats in the back, and don't interfere with my class."

We hurried down the corridor and entered the lecture hall, just as the bell sounded. To my surprise, he proceeded to introduce me as the greatest firsthand authority on glossalalia that he had ever heard. And as he went on, I prayed, "Lord, how can I respond to an introduction like that?" And the Lord said, *Admit that you are an authority on divine glossalalia, but not on demonic glossalalia, for you have never heard any.*

So, I got up and said, "Contrary to what your professor has just told you, I am not an authority on glossalalia. What I *am* is an authority on divine glossalalia. I've heard it said that there is such a thing as demonic glossalalia. I know nothing about that; I've never heard it."

And with that I launched in, and in the course of my lecture, I mentioned that I was occasionally challenged to demonstrate my prayer language, but I never did — unless I had first informed my audience what was happening, and why, for the Apostle warned us not to speak in tongues before the unlearned, or the unbeliever. When I reached the end of my talk, their professor asked for a demonstration.

I started to shake my head, and he said, "My class may not be believers, but do you hold them to be still unlearned?"

I smiled, "If they are still ignorant, they were too dumb to listen."

"Then can you give us a demonstration?"

"Oh," I said, "If you ask me to pray."

He thought for a moment. "Well, all right, we need prayer."

"Then call the class to order."

And he did, instructing them, "Let us follow our guest and do whatever he says."

I took a deep breath. "Well," I began, "usually I say 'bow your heads and let us pray'." And looking around, I saw some doing that, and some assuming different attitudes of prayer. From that I knew we had Muslims and all manner of non-believers; it didn't bother me.

"Next," I said, "I'm going to speak to my heavenly Father — and you know who He is to you. But I am going to reverse Paul's sequence: I will speak with understanding first, and then, when I know not what else to say, I will speak with new tongues, in the Spirit."

And so I forged ahead. I prayed in English, thanking the Lord for the professor and his class and this opportunity. I asked God's blessing on the university and then asked the blessing upon the government, and upon the Queen of England, and then I said, "Lord, but there are other needs here that I do not know. And I ask now for the help of the Spirit, for as the Apostle tells us, 'The Spirit will help our infirmities, our ignorance, and He will make intercession, according to the will of God.' And now I pray from my heart in the Spirit." And I began to pray in tongues.

I prayed quite a while, and when I finished, I said, "Amen." The professor looked up, and then got up and said to the class: "Well, I have today learned from this man what I never knew." And he came over to me and took my hand in both of his. "Thank you very much, especially for the prayer at the end, when you prayed in that language. I cannot deny it did something to me. That is real."

As we were walking out, a young girl came up and said, "I'm Jewish, and I've heard the story of the Tower of Babel, but it never had any particular significance. Today, I learned something, and when you prayed in that funny language, something happened inside of me. I don't know how I'll ever be happy, until I have that experience myself."

Another girl added, "Thank God for what I learned today! I'm a Catholic. And now I, too, will never be satisfied until I get that blessing."

Outside the lecture hall, those students who were Pentecostal, clustered around. "What did you *do* to him?"

"What? To whom?"

"To the professor — he has never been that kind to any speaker, let alone a preacher!"

"Well, when you told me before, 'There is a Jewish professor, and he is a dangerous fellow,' I immediately prayed: 'Lord, help me to forgive him and love him,' and I did. I loved him and paralyzed him, so that he couldn't do anything." They laughed — and perhaps learned the most important lesson of that day.

Are tongues divisive?

In 1978, I was based in Switzerland, and was invited to speak at a Jesuit seminary, just outside of Zurich. The president of that institution had invited Protestants and Pentecostals, Lutherans and Charismatics, and Catholic priests from all over northern Switzerland. It was quite a gathering. Just before the meeting, he put me on the spot: "Will you please tell us how you can be so sure that this Charismatic Movement is really uniting the Body of Christ? Because we find that they are tongues-speakers, and tongues is an extremely divisive issue."

"Well," I said, "I've never been asked to speak on that, but I will ask the Lord to help me." And fortunately there was a Pentecostal pastor there who was the best German interpreter I had ever had.

Waiting to be introduced, I sat on that platform, and prayed: "Lord, You told me to agree to it, but I don't know where to begin."

Begin by asking them whether they believe the Church is divided.

So I stood up and said, "Are you all agreed that we do have divisions in Christianity?"

They all agreed.

"And who causes these divisions?"

One rough voice said, "The devil."

"That's just what I expected!" I scolded them. "You blame the devil for everything that you don't understand! Let me show you where division originated," and I read them Genesis 11, the story of Babel. "Here it's clear that there was only one language in the whole world, and they were building a tower, and God said, 'The fact that they can communicate with each other makes them so powerful, they can do anything they've a mind to. We must break this unity.' And the way He broke it was by introducing different languages. That's where the divisions began, not with the devil."

But now, here came the other question: "Why did the same thing happen on the Day of Pentecost that had happened at the tower of Babel?" That one was easier. "God so loved the world — all nations, all tongues, everybody — that He gave His only begotten Son, that whosoever believed, should not perish but have everlasting life. He sent Jesus to save the world, but the world was divided . . . how to reach them? Nobody could have dreamed that on the Day of Pentecost, the same phenomenon which God had used to divide Man, He would now use to unite him. Jews out of every nation under heaven heard those Galileans speaking languages that they did not know, and they *understood*. Three thousand Jews out of every nation became the body of the Church."

There was surprise and then joy at that observation, and the seminary president exclaimed: "I am convinced! You have given me the strongest Scriptural reason for tongues. From now on, my position will be the opposite from what it has been all these years. I now say I wish every Jesuit would speak in tongues."

What happens when tongues comes into a church?

If, by the grace of God, the gift is accompanied in equal measure by the gift of wisdom, nothing unseemly will happen. A classic example is what happend to Fr. Dennis Bennett, rector of a successful Episcopal church in Van Nuys, California, who was being considered for bishop. Dennis received the Baptism in the Holy Spirit, and he wrote me that when he began to speak in tongues, one of his curates turned against him, and his church was ready to split. But rather than let that happen, he resigned. "Now," he wrote, "I could start a new church, and I believe that some 600 or more (out of a former congregation of 2,000) would come with me. Or some of the Pentecostals who have heard of my difficulty, have invited me to join them. I've heard that you are ecumenically-minded; what would you advise?"

Quickly I wrote back and said: "Whatever you do, don't split the church! It will give you a bad reputation. And if you start an independent church, every speckled bird in the area will join you, and you'll have an impossible congregation. And don't join the Pentecostals, because you'll be up a blind alley. They are already blessed, and you couldn't bless them any more. And your ministry will not fit into their pattern at all. Ask for another parish. But whatever you do, stay in the Episcopal Church. God wants to use you there."

So he went to his bishop, who told him, "If you promise me you will never speak in tongues and never talk about it, I can give you another church, but not as big a congregation, as the one you had."

Dennis said, "That I cannot do. I cannot abandon this new life of prayer."

"Well then, I cannot help you."

So he ended going to Seattle, to seek the advice of a bishop who was an old friend. This man said, "Dennis, I cannot give you a big church. But I am willing to give you a big challenge: there is a church downtown that used to be *the* church in Seattle. It has gone down. They are supposed to still have a hundred members on the membership list, but only ten or twenty people attend. What's more, the Diocese has been supporting them, and they are now $15,000 in debt to us. We have decided that we cannot afford to keep it open more than another two or three months. I'll give you that church, and I don't care if you get everybody to speak in tongues, as long as the church revives. You are free to run it as you choose, and I will guarantee your support for some months."

Dennis accepted. And the next time I was scheduled to pass through Seattle, on my way to Vancouver, I called him ahead of time. "I have a couple of hours to lay over at the airport. Why don't you come out?" When I landed, here was Dennis with a handful of people. They had engaged a room, and we had a meeting right at the airport! It was the first time I had actually met Dennis, and it was wonderful. On my way back, I stopped in again, and now there were twenty people.

The church continued to grow. They were able to repay the $15,000, and to start paying Dennis a salary. They were thriving, but now Dennis had a new problem: although most of his congregation was getting the Baptism, hardly any were exercising the gifts of the Spirit. "Oh," I said, "so now you're becoming Pentecostal, eh?"

"What do you mean?"

"In too many Pentecostal churches, when people recieve the Baptism, especially the women, you never hear from them again. There's no opportunity for them to minister or to have any manifestations."

"What would you advise?"

"The Church in Jerusalem was not in the synagogue or the temple; they were house to house. Why don't you develop house meetings — cells? Divide your congregation into ten groups of twenty."

"Won't that develop cliques?"

"Not if you make sure that no group has a leader who wants to be its pastor. *You* be the pastor, and whoever is the leader of each group must report to you, and you must not be the leader of any group. Moreover, you must not be the pastor of only the Charismatics. You are the pastor of all the sinners that come to the church. You are the shepherd."

And so they began, and the church flourished. It grew, until it was bigger than the one Dennis had had in Van Nuys, and probably the most alive Episcopal congregation in America.

Is the tongues-speaker supposed to interpret his own message?

There is a group in Switzerland that always asks: "Why is it that we have one mouth and two ears, and yet we talk twice as much as we listen?" It is time that we listened — listened to the Lord. For how often people talk in tongues and never stop to listen what the answer is going to be. That's why the Apostle said: "Let him that speaks in a tongue, pray, that he may interpret." That means the speaker in tongues is to *listen* to get the interpretation of what he has said; otherwise, the Church cannot be blessed. Of course, the tongues-speaker sometimes lacks the courage to give the interpretation of what he has just spoken, even if it has come to his mind. And there are people who have a special ministry in the field of interpretation. But unfortunately, we have made a rule of the exception, hoping that someone else will get and give the interpretation.

3

OF PROPHECY, HEALING, AND OTHER GIFTS

When one receives the Baptism in the Holy Spirit, he may also receive spiritual gifts other than the gift of tongues. Here, the author shares wisdom gained from more than half a century of dealing with such gifts.

How did you receive the gift of prophecy?

Young and newly-baptized in the Spirit, I was thrilled — but soon wanted more. "Lord," I said, "why should I limit myself to tongues and interpretation, when I could edify the church with prophecy?" And so, one day I simply took courage and spoke out loud the words that seemed to be forming inside.

"Well," our congregation said, "David, now you've got *three* gifts — tongues, interpretation, and prophecy. Use them or you'll lose them." And *everybody* said it, for that was the accepted teaching, back then. Well, I tried, but they wouldn't function. I had nothing to say. I even considered quoting Scripture in resonant King James language and pretending it was prophesy, as I had heard others do — "Thus saith the Lord!" But I could not bring myself to do that. So despite their urging, I remained silent.

But in private, I cried out to the Lord: "What is wrong?" And then I remembered something which I had just recently learned about our translation of the Bible: where they were not certain of the exact meaning of a word, they put it in italics. That included the word *gifts* in the first verse of I Corinthians 12. Aha! Six verses further on it said: "But the manifestation of the Spirit is given to every man to profit withal."

"That does it!" I exclaimed. "It's only a manifestation of a gift. It is not a gift that I'm using; it is a manifestation of the Spirit, Who is using me to impart it." And then I discovered what Paul wrote to the believers in Rome (1:11): "I long to see you, that I may impart to you some spiritual gift." I saw then, that while I could impart gifts, as the Spirit moved me, I could not use those gifts, because they were not mine to use. They were always by the Spirit and of the Spirit, the same Spirit. This began to help me to get back in tune again, and to dare to speak out in prophecy.

How do you feel about prophecy today?

I don't specifically prophesy anymore, because when I'm preaching, it's all intermixed — sometimes it's prophetic, sometimes a word of knowledge or a word of wisdom. As far as I'm concerned, Joel used the word *prophecy* for the whole lot. That is why you will never hear me say "Thus saith the Lord"; the Spirit gives me the words, or the thought, or the sentence. I came to this realization, talking to people who came to me for advice. What I thought I was giving them was a word of wisdom, but later on, when they came back, they would say: "You know, you gave us a prophecy. We remembered what you said, and it happened exactly the same way, even the very words that you said, came up again."

I did ask the Lord about it once, and He said: *Why do you want to know?*

"Oh, just to know what is working."

You are ministering to many people, and you do not know what is in their hearts — what to one is a word of wisdom, to another is a word of knowledge, and to a third is a prophetic word. What they get is what they need.

And so I stopped bothering about what I was delivering.

Are tongues plus interpretation equal to prophecy?

No, prophecy edifies the church. Tongues and interpretation also edify the church, but it isn't the same thing. What I have heard in Pentecostal ranks is not interpretation of prayer, though it often seems to be; it is prophecy. Dennis Bennett once asked me: "David, what am I to do? I now have a church full of educated, learned men, and they are observant. They question how it is possible that somebody can speak a few words in tongues, and here comes another who gives a two-minute interpretation?"

I said to him, "Now listen: Suppose you hear me pray in tongues, and I happen to pray in a language that you understand. I say, 'Father, this audience is divided into people who need edification, to be built up, others who need exhortation to minister, still others who need Your comforting in their troublesome lives. Speak a word that will edify them, exhort them, and comfort them.' There, I prayed for three things, or rather, the Spirit, through me, made intercession for the audience. Now what would you say if someone then spoke a prophetic word that fulfilled all three requests — edifying, exhorting, and comforting?"

Dennis smiled. "I'd say that was a pretty quick answer to prayer."

"Yes," I agreed, "but it is not interpretation; it's an answer to the prayer in the Spirit."

Can you give an example of the three gifts in operation?

The Lord gave just such an example while I was teaching in a big Pentecostal church in Vancouver. The pastor was a younger man, and as I was speaking, to my surprise and the congregation's he did something which they had never heard him do: he stood up and burst out in tongues. I stopped, because the Apostle said that if anything is revealed to another, let the first speaker hold his peace. So I held my peace, and when he stopped, I waited expectantly for him to give the interpretation. But instead of him or anyone else giving it, a dear old man, sitting in the front row, began to prophesy with a feeble, little voice. Quickly I took out my pen and made notes of what he said.

Hardly anyone, other than those in front, could hear him, and the audience sat there, dumb. Then, way back on the left, a man stood up and with the same strong voice which the pastor had used, he began to praise the Lord, and thank the Lord. And I wrote down what *he* said.

When he finished, there was quiet. "Folks," I said, "I've been speaking to you under the unction of the Holy Spirit, trying to teach you His ways. Now normally, the Holy Spirit does not interrupt Himself, but here He has just given us a perfect demonstration."

I gestured to the old man in the front row. "This dear brother — you in the back couldn't hear what he was saying, but he was prophesying. Only it was out of order. He should have waited for the interpretation of your pastor's message in tongues. Prophecy can always wait; it'll come out at the right time. But this brother, when he heard the tongues, was so blessed that he was over-anxious to give his prophecy."

I pointed to the man in the back. "Now that brother there — he has given us the interpretation of the pastor's prayer, which was intercession for the congregation. If, after the pastor had spoken, his prayer had been interpreted, and then the prophecy had been given, that would have been in perfect order."

I looked around at them, and they were paying close attention. "Incidentally, this demonstration which the

Lord has provided, also shows the difference between tongues and interpretation, and prophecy. Your pastor spoke in tongues, and 'he that speaketh in a tongue, speaks not to men, but to God.' Prophecy is the Spirit of God speaking to men, and its purpose, too, is to edify the church. But his prophecy," and here I read from my notes, " 'If we will prayerfully abide by the Scriptures, we will learn from the Holy Spirit, how to pray and praise the Lord' — instead of teaching us, merely told us what the Holy Spirit would do."

I pointed again to the man in the back. "That brother, who evidently didn't hear him, came forth with what I would call the perfect interpretation. Like your pastor, he was speaking to God, not to the congregation, and the combination of tongues and interpretation are together edifying to this audience. But you could not be edified by prophecy that you couldn't hear."

The audience rejoiced, and one man stood up and asked, "Why don't we get this kind of teaching? Why do we let all kinds of manifestations come, and nobody tells us what is happening?"

"Listen," I replied, "I don't always tell you what I'm doing, and I usually don't know beforehand what I'm going to do. But I do bring a word of wisdom, and also a word of knowledge. When it's the latter, and it hits the nail on the head, you may think: 'Who told him about me?' But it is the word of wisdom that will liberate you from your problem. Because the wisdom is the escape from the knowledge that brought you under conviction or reproved you."

I thought for a moment, then added: "What you usually hear after tongues is not interpretation but prophecy. I have no objection to that, as long as it is edifying to the church, and you don't call everything that follows tongues, interpretation."

How about designated tongues-speakers and interpreters?

In a Pentecostal community, that is a tragedy, because no one else will be used of the Lord. They would not dare. I was speaking in a church in South Africa, where I found that they had an official speaker in tongues and an official interpreter. And so, the first night, as I came to the conclusion of my message, a sister broke loose and spoke in tongues, and a man to my right gave the interpretation; these were the recognized ones. But all he did was confirm what I had said, and I thought: that was unnecessary; why should he bother? That was not what Scripture says is the purpose of interpretation — or prophecy, for that matter.

The next night, the same thing happened — only now, he corrected my message. In that instant, I saw what was going on, and I openly challenged him: "Last night, I heard what you call interpretation, and it approved what I preached. Tonight, you have the indecency to correct. When I preach, I am under the anointing of the Holy Spirit, and the Holy Spirit does not correct me from someone who's a listener and who ought to be listening."

But far from listening now, from the redness of his face and the look he was giving me, he was getting angrier by the moment. "You may not have liked what I said," I went on, "and you surely will not like what I am going to say now. And let me make this clear: I am speaking to you now, as the General Secretary of this movement. You, sister," and I turned to her, "do not speak in tongues in this meeting for the rest of the week. And you, brother, do not interpret again. You two are through. I want the Lord to use other members of this body; you have controlled this church long enough by your so-called official ministry."

In the stunned silence that followed, the two of them got up and left — and a lot of the congregation also left. In their eyes, I had grieved the Holy Spirit — so much so that the next night, hardly anyone came to the meeting. "What do we do now?" the anxious pastor asked.

"Well, the week isn't over yet; we'll go visiting."

"Visiting? Who?"

"The first person I want to see," I smiled, "is that sister who spoke in tongues."

And so, the pastor took me there, and I sat down with her and gently said: "Sister, I did not have any kind of feeling that you were out of order last night. You spoke sweetly and lovingly in tongues. But the interpreter is a man who disturbed me both nights. Can you tell me, before the Lord, that he gives the correct interpretations? Does your spirit blend with his spirit?"

At first, she said nothing, but then she could stand it no longer and blurted out: "No! I've been going through hell with this situation here! But he threatened me in many kinds of ways. I must speak, he said, so he can interpret, and he says just what he wants to. I don't agree with either what he did or what he said, and my spirit resents the man now!"

The pastor comforted her, and I took her hand. "Thank you, for telling us the truth. Now I want to say to you: I think the Lord has sent me here to help your church and to help you. For you can still be a great blessing."

That lady was older than I was, and I saw her again, the last time I was in South Africa. She was still alive, and what a blessing she was! She said that she would never, never forget in eternity what I had done for her, and looked forward to thanking the Lord in person for it.

And now we went to see this man. He was not home. And we could not get ahold of him anywhere. He did not want to meet me at all. Later, at a board meeting long after I had left, it became known that the man in question had been living for a long time in darkness. Here, then, was a case which demonstrated how an official designation allowed somebody to live crooked and still have a position. There was a happy ending to that story; when the whole thing came out into the light, the man was forgiven, and there was peace. And to the delight of the pastor, who had blamed himself for the lack of progress in his church, the faithful stuck by him, and now that the darkness had been banished, blessings followed upon blessings.

So, whenever just one or two people are singled out to exercise spiritual gifts, it is not right. I have ten fingers, and each finger has its ministry; if I allow just one finger to function, the others will atrophy and eventually become paralyzed.

Can self get mixed in with prophecy?

All too easily — prophecy can be a tremendous ego-trap. And the sad thing is, when one has that problem, he cannot tell when the Spirit leaves off, and self takes over.

For example, in Wales, where the Apostolic Church thrives on prophecy, I discovered that they had a local prophet, who prophesied only in local prayer meetings, and a county prophet, who prophesied in pastors' or circle meetings. Similarly, there was a national prophet, and even an international prophet. The latter, I discovered, was definitely the longest winded of them all, who would go on and on and on. Nobody could remember what he said, unless they taped it, and I doubted that they would ever listen to it again.

What level of importance should prophecy have?

There was a difficulty with prophecy in the early days of the Pentecostal Movement, when they began to find that these prophecies were really true. They began to put them on a level with Scripture, saying "It was taught to us by prophecy." This was eventually carried to such an extreme that some churches would do nothing, unless it was directed by prophecy. Such a church was having a farewell banquet for their pastor who had a prophetic ministry and who was retiring, and they sent me an invitation. In the letter, they explained that the function would be arranged entirely by prophecy. Needless to say, I regretfully declined.

I do not believe that the prophet goes before the apostle, or that the prophet has greater credibility than a man of God who does not happen to have a prophetic ministry. If the latter is a good preacher or a good teacher, then he is as much under the unction of the Holy Spirit as the fellow who is prophesying. Let the prophet speak, and let the elders judge. For the prophet is never free to speak just as he pleases or do just as he likes. The elders must examine the situation and exercise control, for prophecy can be a great and wonderful blessing, but like all other good things, if you have too much of it, then you get sick.

I will never forget what Charles Heatley used to say, when the students of his Bible class used to beg him for more. "No," he would say, "No more. Too much chocolate makes you sick."

Can you say a word about grace?

In Ephesians 4, we learn "But unto every one of us, is given grace according to the measure of the gift of Christ." The Holy Spirit has gifts, but Christ also gives gifts, and some are shocked when I say that. But "He gives grace according to the measure of the gifts of Christ." And what are those gifts of Christ? Well, we read that "He gave some apostles, some prophets, some evangelists, and some pastors and teachers, for the perfecting of the saints, for the work of the ministry, for the edifying of the Body of Christ."

And when we turn to Romans 12:23, we find a little more, for here Paul says that you surrender to Him: "I beseech you, brethren, by the mercies of God, that ye present your bodies a living sacrifice wholly acceptable unto God, which is your reasonable service" — your service, your ministry. "And be not conformed to this world, but be ye transformed by the renewing of your mind, that ye may prove what is that good and acceptable and perfect will of God." All that goes with a ministry, not gifts.

Then he says, "I say unto you, through the grace given to me, to every man that is among you, not to think of himself more highly than he ought, but to think soberly according as God has dealt every man the measure of faith." There is a measure of faith, and according to that measure of faith He has dealt you, you then can minister. But you will need grace. And if you think of the evangelist or the apostle as someone who establishes churches and works, he needs a lot more grace, because he's going to meet with conflict.

Which is why Paul wrote to Timothy in that first epistle: "Wherefore I put thee in remembrance that thou stir up the gift of God which is in thee, by the putting on of my hands." Now, here is a gift of God, and what did He give Timothy? "For God has not given us the spirit of fear, but of power, and of love, and of a sound mind." That means that Timothy received the Baptism under the hands of Paul — "the gift of God that you received by the putting on of my hands."

He reminds Timothy, then, to "be faithful to the gift that's in thee, by the putting on of the hands of the presbytery (that's his ordination) and given to thee by prophecy — and the laying on of hands of the elders (that is a ministry)."

So Timothy can speak of three gifts: he's got the gift of God, the Holy Spirit Himself; he's got the gift of Christ, a ministry; and he can manifest gifts of the Spirit. But not all the same kind of a gift — to manifest tongues and interpretation, you need to have a meek and yielded spirit.

What about miracles?

In the beginning, they used to make me mad. In 1916, when the Lord saved me, I saw these black Africans doing all sorts of miracles, and I thought: How can they do them so easily? I decided that it was because they were uneducated; they simply didn't know that you couldn't just ask God for a miracle and believe that He would do it, and that that was all there was to it. I was so wise at age twelve, and their faith was so simple, it confounded me.

I particularly remember one Sunday morning meeting conducted in a shed before there was a lovely church building on this mission station. My father was building a house for missionaries, and in the meantime, we were living in African huts. It was warm in the meeting, and we boys were sitting next to Mother and Father, as always. We had just finished a hymn, when an old black lady who was the wife of one of the chiefs, came in and said that on her way to the meeting, she had stopped at the hut of a certain old sister, who was very ill; the chief's wife thought she was dying — could we pray for her?

So we all joined hands and prayed for her, and as we did, the chief's wife got up and walked out — and the congregation, including my father and the missionaries, followed her. Wanting to see what was going to happen next, I ran along.

When they got to the sick woman's hut, one of the missionaries and Daniel, an old African evangelist, went in, as the rest stayed outside and sang choruses in their native language. All of a sudden, out of the hut came the lady

who had been sick, and she was *dancing!* She danced all
the way to the church, and what rejoicing there was!
"Jesus is alive! He's proved it again!"

To a young boy, such a miracle made a deep impression. It was just like the New Testament, and so it meant
that that Catholic church down there, the one which had
been saying we were of the devil, were themselves of the
devil. And the Presbyterian and Reformed churches?
Well, they did not have the full Gospel, not like we did.
But now my question was: how do *I* do miracles? I
prayed, "Lord, I'm twelve years old, and you were
twelve when you said, 'I must be about my Father's
business.' How can I learn the secret of miracles?"

Begin at the beginning — that was all He seemed to
say. But what did it mean? Finally, I decided that it
meant the beginning of Jesus' supernatural ministry,
when He performed His first miracle. It was at the wedding in Cana, when He turned the water into wine. Aha!
And how did that miracle begin? With His mother telling
the servant: "Whatsoever He says to you, do it." And I
took that as a cue: if you want to see miracles, you must
do *exactly* what Jesus says. And then it struck me: how
faithful these Africans were to believe what they heard,
and to follow that line of healing!

Are miracles for today?

Of course! But there is today an over-emphasis on
miracles of physical healing, and not enough on the
miracle of salvation and spiritual healing. All the
miraculous ministry of Jesus did not save Israel. His
miracle of increasing the loaves and the fish drew more

multitudes than all the healings. Yet when He promised them His body to eat and His blood to drink, they went away disgusted.

Miracles are *not* what will save the world, or bring the world to repentance. If miracles *could* save, then the miracles that God did in Egypt should have saved Israel. But none of the miracles caused the Egyptians to let Israel go free. Not one. In the end, it was the blood of a little lamb on the doorpost that made the division between Egyptians and Israelites. God said: "When I see the blood, I will pass over you." Is it any wonder that John introduced Jesus as the Lamb of God that takes away the sin of the world? For sinners to get saved, it is Jesus, the Lamb of God, whom we need to uplift. As He said, "If I be lifted up from the earth, I will draw all men unto me."

How do you respond to those who would de-mythologize the Bible?

I offer to help them. For I certainly don't want anyone misled, or believing anything in the Bible which isn't true. I once met with Heinrich Ott, the eminent theologian who was Barth's protege, until he got tangled up with Bultmann. Stealing a march on him, I led off by informing him that my ministry was de-mythologizing the Scriptures — taking out everying that wasn't true.

"You *what*?" he exclaimed.

"Now don't act dumb," I replied. "You've studied under Bultmann, haven't you?" He nodded. "Well, Bultmann's position — and yours, too, apparently — is that many things in the Bible could not possibly be true, because they cannot be found in the Church today." Again, he nodded.

"Ah," I smiled, "there's your mistake: you are judging the Bible by the Church, instead of the Church by the Bible. The things that you and Bultmann tell me are myths, I have been able to produce in the 20th century, and I can produce millions of witnesses who have had the same experiences that Peter and James and John had on the Day of Pentecost. I myself experienced it in 1918. I have taken all your so-called 'myths' and made them 20th-century reality, just like that — and some even greater."

He shook his head. "I never thought of that."

"Well," I concluded, "I wish *you* would de-mythologize the Bible, as I do, by making all the myths come true."

Haven't you personally experienced Philip's miracle in Acts 8?

Yes, although I seldom speak of it. But since Dennis Bennett persuaded me to let him and Rita tell the story, I don't mind repeating it. Years ago, in South Africa, a brother preached a sermon on Sunday, in which he claimed that he was sufficiently sanctified to be out of reach of the Enemy. "I live above sin," he said, "where no devil can ever touch me."

The next morning, he went berserk, and I knew what had happened: the Enemy had risen to his challenge, and God had permitted it. As it happened, I was helping two other men to reconcile that morning, when the Holy Spirit told me to go to the stricken brother's house. I told the men that I was going to run there as fast as I could, and that they were welcome to follow. I went out the gate, put one foot down — and was standing on the doorsill of the stricken man's house!

Looking around, I couldn't believe it. "How did I get here?" I murmured. "Nothing happened; I'm here in the twinkling of an eye!"

Hearing noises inside, I went in, and noticed a Bible, lying on a table. Picking it up, I went into the bedroom, where four men were holding the brother down. "Let him go!" I commanded, and as they did, he rose up and came straight for me. I held up the Bible and declared, "On the authority of this word, I rebuke you!"

He fell back on the bed, as if I'd shot him. I walked over to him. "Satan, in Jesus' name, I command you to leave this man, get out, and never come back again."

When I said that, a sister standing at the end of the bed, gave a scream, and when I asked her what was the matter, she cried, "A huge serpent crawled out from under the bed and has gone out the window! He went right by me!"

I turned to the brother, who was calm now. "What happened?" I asked him.

"Something had coiled himself around me and was choking me, which was why I got violent. Then, when you came in the door, I thought you were the devil — "

"Because that's what he wanted you to think," I explained.

Just then, the two men who had been with me, arrived. "How long has he been here?" they asked the others.

"About 20 minutes," someone replied.

"But that's impossible! We left when he did, and it took us 20 minutes to get here!" They paused and looked at one another, and then at me. One said, "We were following you, as you headed for the gate, and we heard it click behind you. But when we got to it ourselves, you were nowhere to be seen." They paused. "What happened?"

"I think I was transported," I said softly, "there's no other explanation. But for goodness sake, don't talk about it." For I knew of a black African who had been transported, and his people made an idol out of him. The others respected my wishes, and for that reason even today I seldom speak of it.

How do you handle healing in your meetings?

I never allow people to lay hands on others for the Baptism, but for healing I wish everyone would lay on hands, because, as He said, "These signs shall follow them that believe in my Name, they shall lay hands on the sick and they shall recover."

I was in a pastors' meeting in Switzerland, and they asked me if I would have a healing meeting. I asked if there were sick people there, and when I was told that there was, I announced that there would be a healing meeting that afternoon, and for all the sick to be brought.

After the meeting opened, I asked, "How many of you here now believe in Jesus' name? You believe He's Saviour? You believe He's the Healer? You believe He's Almighty? He's God?" All hands up. "Aha! That's wonderful! Now I see that nobody needs to go out of this meeting sick." And then I gave them the ground rules: "I'm not laying hands on anybody; I'm not the pastor, or an elder of this church. But you are." And now I looked around and asked, "Where are all the sick people?" Quite a number of hands went up. I then addressed the rest: "Will all you believers lay hands on these people?"

But as they moved to do so, one pastor began to shout: "Oh, Glory to God, I . . . I'm healed!"

I said, "Well, praise the Lord! That's wonderful!"

He looked around. "But four brethren who laid hands on me — which one healed me?"

"None of them," I explained, "none of them could. Jesus healed you."

"Yes, I know," he said impatiently, "but who has the gift?"

I looked at him sternly. "Nobody has a gift to heal. Read the Bible: there are gifts *of* healing, never gifts *to* heal. And a gift of healing is for sick people. The only people who can receive a gift *of* healing are sick people, and if they get the gift of healing, they'll be well. I have found there's one thing better than a gift of healing, and that's divine health. You don't get sick."

I've also found out, that if I have failed God somewhere, and I humble myself and confess, I don't get sick. For "He forgiveth all thine iniquities, He healeth all thy diseases." But if I am guilty of any kind of iniquity, even jealousy, that renders me vulnerable. There are some things that people don't think are sin, but which are. They blame the devil for them, when it's only the work of the flesh. But that is for another chapter — the next one.

4

THE DARK SIDE

As a Christian seeks to go deeper in his walk with the Spirit, invariably he will have a personal confrontation with the forces of darkness. God permits the Enemy to harass us, so that we will learn by firsthand experience who is stronger, Satan or Christ. We can read this and be told this and believe it in our heads, but until we walk through it, with Christ as our champion and defender, we will not know in our hearts that He is always victor. At the crest of the Charismatic Movement, the practice of the exorcism of demons was introducing fear into the Christian's life. In most churches this was generally discredited, but recently it has re-surfaced, and is once again taking the Christian's focus off the Lord, and placing it on the devil and his henchmen. Needless to say, the author has some strong feelings about this.

I object to people forever equating the gift of discerning of spirits with discerning of devils. They spend all their time looking for demons — the devil keeps them so busy looking for him, they don't see the Lord. Personally, I say that I don't need the help of the Holy Spirit to discern the devil. I recognize him at a distance. I know his roar already. He is not such a mystical fellow as all that. Some people think of him as supernatural, but I say he is *un*natural. Only God is supernatural. But the devil suggests unnatural things to us — and it does not take much discernment to tell who's doing the suggesting! But you do need discernment when you come to the work of the Lord, and to spiritual things. We find the best example of true spiritual discernment in I Corinthians, where Paul shows how dangerous is "*not* discerning the Lord's body." (I Corinthians 12:13)

As to discernment of the Spirit, there are those who say: "But it said spirits."

"Yes," I reply, "Revelation speaks of the seven spirits of God, and when Paul described the spiritual gifts which the Lord gives, he wrote: 'to another working of miracles, to another prophesy, to another discerning spirits.' It is plural, but it does not say *evil* spirits."

There is a lack of discernment in the Church today, because pastors have not come to recognize that discernment is discerning the mind of the Spirit, and *not* devils. Look at the Body of Christ, whose members are supposed to care for one another, and so on. *That* is where discernment comes in: what is troubling your neighbor?

One man whom I believe has manifested a remarkable ministry of discernment is Demos Shakarian. The founder of the Full Gospel Businessmen's Fellowship, he is not a pastor or a preacher, but time and again, I have seen Full Gospel meetings come to a dead halt and deteriorate into hopeless confusion — and Demos would discern what the block was and know exactly what to do, to enable the Spirit to move again. Seeing that he needed to step in, he would stand and gently say, "Isn't Jesus wonderful?" And then he would look around and point to a man he could not have known, and describe him and ask him to stand. "Now, brother, I believe the Lord wants you to give us a word of testimony." And invariably, he would strike the right man at the right time. He could not introduce him, because he did not know his name. But the Lord knew, and Demos was obedient. That is an example of the gift of discernment, and how it edifies and builds up the body of believers.

Can a Christian have a demon?

I also object to people blaming the devil for everything. Sometimes I will say to them: "You think you're full of devils, but you're just full of yourself, that's all." When that question was put to a friend of mine, Judson Cornwall, he said: "Christians can have anything they want."

Now, here we have this great move today of exorcism.

How did the exorcism ministry get started?

The tradition of exorcism is built on one Scripture only — one that has a false punctuation in it. Mark 16:17 reads: "These signs shall follow them that believe. In my name they shall cast out demons."

"These signs will follow them that believe" — believe what? When you take out the punctuation (which is not

in the original Greek and has been arbitrarily inserted by
subsequent translators), it reads: "These signs shall
follow them that believe *in my name*, then they shall
expel — not cast out — other people's demons." They
shall expel the demons, because the Lord says that the
stronger man (Jesus) comes in and casts out the other.
(Luke 11:20-26, I Corinthians 1:25-29, also I John 4:4,
and Hebrews 2:14-18.)

And so began the tragedy that results in brethren exor-
cizing people, making them think that they have been
helped. But I have had to deal with too many who later
came back and said: "I was helped for a few days, and
then it got ten times worse than it was before."

I said, "It's because they did not first get you to believe
in Jesus as Saviour and make your commitment to Him, by
faith in His name. Had you done so, you would have found
that there was no devil within; you would have expelled
him. You would have, in effect, become your own exorcist.

One time, I was sitting in a meeting that Dennis Bennett arranged. An evangelist had been telling them all the
incidents where Jesus cast out devils. I sat and listened to
him, and when he stopped, I added a few more instances
to his list. Surprised, he asked: "So you *do* believe that
Jesus cast out devils?"

"Yes," I smiled, and then looked at him and said, "but
have you never heard that Jesus died?"

"Of course!"

"Well, after His resurrection, there was no more
exorcism."

"Ah," he said, "but what about His saying 'in My name
you shall cast out devils'?"

I said, "Brother, I'm surprised at you! You, a Bible
scholar, ought to know that there's no punctuation in the
original. The punctuation put there later is wickedly

crooked and wrong, and has built a tradition in Christianity. In some of the infant sprinkling churches, they even exorcise that poor little child, as if there were a devil already there.

"And now mothers are being accused — I have heard them preach and say: 'If a mother has a temper when her children are being naughty, she has a demon in her.' She's demonized! And what about the naughty child? Oh, he's demonized too! So the mothers begin casting out devils, instead of teaching their children to love Jesus. It is a shocking thing that has happened with this so-called "deliverance ministry."

I turned to the speaker and said: "On Calvary, Jesus destroyed him that had the power of death, that is, the devil. In the second chapter of Hebrews, verse 17, it *says* the devil! He destroyed him! And delivered those that were in fear of death all their life. Bound by fear of death. Now *there* is deliverance! The deliverance is at the cross of Calvary — there, where Jesus destroyed the devil, and destroyed him so perfectly that he could not hold Him in death. In Resurrection, He ruined the devil's power over death, and brought life."

I turned to them. "We say we've got that life. Then how come we still harbor devils, and we still fear death? The only people that I have exorcised are people that are demented. They are absolutely hopeless — you can't even get them to say the Lord's Prayer. In such cases, I'll take authority over the devil, because that person hasn't got even a mind to surrender to Christ. Backslidden Christians, I bring back to Calvary."

I went back to my chair, saying, "There is all my teaching on, not exorcism, but expulsion — expelling the devil."

The evangelist nodded. "I must admit, David is right. The word 'cast out' there is not the pure translation of what's in the original. It is 'expel'."

I said, "Then why do you let a false text like that become tradition, not only in historic churches but now even in Pentecostal ranks?"

Will you go on challenging "Exorcists"?

Probably not. I was one of the speakers in a Methodist Charismatic Conference, and in the morning there had been so much rejoicing and praising the Lord, and shouting hallelujah, it was like a youth meeting. Then, that afternoon an Evanglist preached, and as he spoke, the joy of the morning vanished; in its place there came a sense of gloom and widespread apprehension. When he finished and invited his audience to come forward for deliverance, about 70% responded. He warned them that they might find that the devil didn't behave very nicely; they might find themselves vomiting.

A doctor, sitting with his wife in front of me, turned to me and in shocked tones asked, "Where are we?"

"Doctor," I replied, "I don't know where you are, but I am safe in the arms of Jesus."

"But what's happened here?" he persisted.

I pointed to the preacher. "That man has created more devils in the minds of these people, than he can cast out."

"What are you going to do?"

I shrugged. "I've either got to go up on that platform and rebuke him, or go out. But if I go up there, my own ministry won't be a blessing. So, I'll just forgive him and forgive the whole thing and walk out." And I did.

How widespread is the resurgence of interest in exorcism?

I was in a meeting of the Charismatic Concerns Committee last May, and here was a man who had just been on the cover of *Charisma*, and he kept on talking about the *'deliverance ministry.'* And when he finished, they opened up for questions, and I said, "I would like to ask the speaker a question, and I'm directing my question to this whole conference — to all of you. I challenge every one of you to give me one text in the Bible that says 'deliverance ministry.' All the ministries are clearly presented in I Corinthians 12, Romans 12, and in Ephesians 4, but there is no mention of a deliverance ministry."

But the man who really shook me was a rising young Baptist preacher, who was to address a conference with a couple of thousand students. The conference was going beautifully, and that afternoon, the glory of the Lord was truly there: the young people clapped, danced, shouted for joy, talked in tongues — it was a little bit of heaven on earth!

But that night, the Baptist preacher held forth. As he built up his message, he grew increasingly somber, until finally he shared how somebody had exorcised him. After his salvation! What a terrible heresy, I thought; he is accusing Jesus of not having saved him from the devil. How could he have had Jesus inside of him if he still had the devil? To me, it was an appalling thing that an educated Baptist preacher like that could have lost the confidence of his salvation. But then, to my horror, he gave an invitation to any who now realized that they needed deliverance, to come forward and he would deliver them. And they flocked forward.

What was I to do? Was I to go to him? To the elders of his denomination? I asked the Lord. *Just pray for him and forgive him. He is my servant, and I will re-direct him.* And He did.

What about exorcism and the baptism?

I know of a brother, so bound by this tradition of exorcism, that when people whom he prayed for to receive the baptism in the Holy Spirit, did not speak in tongues, he would exorcise them! And he also exorcised believers before baptizing them.

I said to him, "When you baptize people in water, what do you do?"

"Oh, I put my arms around them; I'm going to immerse them."

I reminded him of what John the Baptist said, "Like I baptize in water, He'll baptize in the Holy Spirit," and added: "Here you have a person standing right in the arms of Jesus, waiting to be baptized in the Holy Spirit, and you feel you must come and deliver him from the devil, when he's standing in the arms of Jesus! That means that you make Jesus so weak that He cannot deal with the devil!"

What about the age-old excuse, "The devil made me do it"?

In Galatians 6, Paul calls even witchcraft the work of the flesh. He does not accuse the devil of it. At a break during a Lutheran meeting once, they told me of a minister who wanted to talk to me, because he said that if

David du Plessis couldn't help him, he would go out of his mind. Well, he got a hotdog, and I got a hotdog, and we went around the corner, where no one could hear us, or even notice us.

He asked me, "First, when you open up to the Spirit, is it possible that an evil spirit can slip in?"

I looked at him. "Tell me *when* it was that you opened up to the Spirit?"

"When I spoke in tongues."

"You mean, you were not saved before you spoke in tongues? Didn't you know Jesus as your Saviour?"

"Oh, yes, ten years already."

"Then Jesus was already in you. So, when you spoke in tongues, nothing came in." I shook my head. "That's this terrible teaching that tongues is the evidence that you're spirit-filled. You were filled, when you got saved. Now, the Spirit came upon you, like fire, and you were baptized in Him, and that's why you spoke in tongues."

His eyes widened in fear. "But something is terribly wrong, somewhere! Because ever since I've spoken in tongues, I've had suicidal tendencies!"

"Oh, that's wonderful!"

"It is?"

"Yes, because now I think I can tell you what happened. Something said to you: 'Just jump down from a high building, and you will be free from all your troubles.' "

He looked at me, astonished. "How did you know?"

"Don't you know the Scriptures? The same old enemy that took Jesus up on the pinnacle and said to him, 'Jump,' is telling you to jump."

"Oh," he murmured, as understanding came into his eyes.

"Was the devil in Christ? Of course not! There's no devil in you, either. Well, the devil was talking to Jesus, and that's all that's wrong with you: you've been listening to the wrong man!" I put my arm around his shoulder. "He is a liar from the beginning, and he wants you to believe that you're not saved. And he wants you to jump." I looked at him. "Why didn't you jump?"

He frowned, as he recalled the moment. "Funny — something in me stopped me."

"Of course!" I cried. "Don't you know the Scripture: 'Greater is he that is in me than he that is in the world'?"

"Oh, thank God, I don't have a demon!"

"Who told you that you had a demon?"

"A Pentecostal pastor, and he said, 'If these things are in your mind, you ought to be exorcised.'"

Now it was my turn to be astonished. "And you thought *I* would exorcise you?"

"I felt sure you would be able to deliver me somehow."

"Well," I said, "I *have* just delivered you, but *He* is the Way, the Truth, and the Life. And the Truth shall make you free; that is the liberation."

So truth is the antidote?

People who claim to have problems with devils, I can teach the Truth, and the Truth will deliver them. I've delivered far more people by forgiveness than by exorcism — because, after all, the devil gets blamed for a lot of their bitterness. This is the battle I've had, and I have absolute confidence in this approach.

But I have been challenged, too — "How did you develop such faith, that you will not back up?" they ask.

I usually reply: "If it is written in Scripture, then I will not back up one inch for anybody."

5

DIVINE ORDER

For a husband and wife, submitting to one another in harmony is a supernatural undertaking at best, but it is essential, if God's order is to reign in the home — or anywhere else.

"Wives submit yourselves to your own husbands" — now that takes a lot of grace. You really need the Holy Spirit to do that. But He is there, "For the husband is the head of the wife, even as Christ is head of the Church, and He is the Saviour of the Body. Therefore, as the Church is subject unto Christ, so let wives be to their own husbands in everything." I preached this in a meeting, and a minister's wife, who did not like what she had heard, asked me to come to see her.

So I went. I knocked at the front door, and when she opened it, and I went in, I was shocked. Her walls were covered with framed Scriptures, but there wasn't an encouraging text anywhere, only judgments. And facing the front door was the text: "The wicked shall be turned into hell."

"Sister," I asked her, "what is that?"

"Oh," she said, "That is to remind him."

"Who?"

"My husband."

"But," I said, "he's a preacher."

"Yes, but he's not saved; I'm sure of that."

"And you want him to go to hell?"

"No, I warn him."

I said, "Put that in the fire, and put in its place: 'Jesus loves you anyhow.' " I thought for a moment. "By the way, does he come in the front door?"

"No, now that you mention it, he never comes in the front door."

"Neither will I again, if you don't take that text off!" And I tried to show her that this was not the way to draw someone into the Kingdom. She was an educated, cultured woman, and as we talked, she grew angry. "You mean, I must submit to this husband, who, for all his education and theology, I am not sure is even a Christian?"

I could understand his difficulty: his wife had become a Pentecostal and now had a typical Pentecostal attitude toward non-Pentecostals. (So many Pentecostals still think that they are the only people who are right.) We talked for some time, and I don't know what happened, but as I was leaving, she said, "Will you come again? My husband will want to meet you."

I did come back, and the three of us had lunch together. All the condemning texts were gone, and I had a suspicion that he knew that I had something to do with this. So we had a wonderful conversation. Later on, I got a long-distance call from her: "You said I must submit to my husband in everything. Now he wants me to go with him to see a movie."

"Well," I said, "what's the matter?"

"I don't want to see movies."

"You don't have to look. Why not sit beside him, and pray for him and close your eyes?"

"I must go?"

"Of course."

"All right, I'll go, but I'll tell the Lord that you said to."

"I'll take the blame gladly." I did not hear any report, and the next time I saw her, I asked her what happened.

"Oh," she exclaimed, "it was wonderful! It was all about Martin Luther, and I so enjoyed it."

"And did you apologize to your husband?"

"Why?"

"Because you had miserable feelings that he was taking you to a sinful movie, and he's too much of a gentleman to take a Christian like you to such a movie. He knew that you would be blessed by seeing it, and he wanted to treat you to a good blessing." I laughed; this poor lady was having a hard time with me.

Another time, she came to me. "You told me I must go always anywhere my husband wanted to go." I nodded. "They are now having a great party, a banquet, and he wants me to go. All the theologians and so on, will be there."

"Well, of course you go."

"But I don't want to. These people take liquor, and strong drink, and so on."

"Well, can't you take a soda?"

"Yes, but I don't want to be with them."

"Sister, what's the matter with you? The Lord is giving you a fishing pond, where you could fish." I paused. "You may meet somebody else who is in the same predicament that you think you are in."

"Well, I'll go. But I'll tell the Lord that you said so."

The next morning on the phone, she told me how it went. "You must have spoken prophetically! I found the wife of a politician who was in exactly the same predicament. We found ourselves a nice corner, and spent the evening together."

"And you never mixed with the people?"

"No."

"Then," I replied sharply, "you are a disgrace to Jesus. Jesus mixed with those people. He ate with them. And He did not suffer because of that, even though they called Him a glutton and a wine-bibber. Why, you must have, with the other lady, groaned together over your miserable husbands. That's no honor to Jesus."

Some time later, I was invited to preach in a church near by, and she asked her husband, "Can I have the car? David du Plessis is preaching tonight, and I want to go to that meeting."

"David du Plessis's preaching? Then I'll take you." And that man came to a pentecostal meeting. (You can win them, if they know you love them and forgive them.)

Over the years, I sent my newsletters to her. And now here I get a letter from her. Her husband has passed away. But before he died, he asked her to sit by his bed and read to him from the Scriptures. Finally, one day, he said, "David du Plessis sends you his newsletters, and you sometimes left them in the kitchen, and I had an idea you wanted me to read them. I did. Do you keep them?"

"Yes, I have a file."

"Please bring them here and read to me what he writes."

She read to him from my newsletters, the little

messages that I have there. And when she had finished, he said, "Thank you very much." He laid back, and she thought he was going to sleep. All of a sudden, she heard him say: "Yes, Lord, I'm coming," and he was gone, with a smile on his face.

She ended her letter by thanking me for helping her to be a blessing instead of a hindrance in his Christian life. That is what I call submission to your husband.

And what about husbands?

"Husbands, love your wives, even as Christ loved the church and gave Himself for it, that He might sanctify and cleanse it with the washing of water by the Word, that He might present it to Himself a glorious church, not having spot or wrinkle or any such thing, but that it should be holy and without blemish. So ought men to love their wives even as their own bodies. He that loveth his wife, loveth himself. For no man ever yet hated his own flesh, but nourisheth and cherisheth it, even as the Lord the church."

A husband, as the head of the house, has an assignment to make his wife beautiful. The Church is not so beautiful. The Church is made up of sinners, saved by grace, but Jesus beautifies it. See how He brings us into favor. This, then, is what a husband ought to mean to a good wife.

Ladies have said to me, "But how can I submit to a husband like that? I don't know whether he even loves me."

"Well," I answer, "submit until he can't help loving you."

Husbands say: "You don't know my wife; she's a cat."

"Love her into submission." This is what I call walking in the Spirit. And it's not only in church; you need to be in the Spirit at home. You need to be in the spirit before your children, because they will watch your life.

Walking in the Spirit is a 24-hour-a-day business. You cannot just switch it on, when you want to. You cannot say that you are in the Spirit, if you are only spiritual in church. You take Him home. The meeting will be over, the retreat will end. You can never say at the door: "Goodbye, Holy Ghost. We'll see you next meeting." He does not stay there; He goes with you.

He does more than that; on Monday, He goes to work with you. And you can't say, "Goodbye, honey, see you tonight; goodbye, Holy Spirit, I'll be home this evening." He goes with you, because you need Him. For the Apostle says: "Servants, be obedient to them that are your masters after the flesh with fear and trembling in singleness of your heart, as unto Christ."

One fellow asked me, "You mean, I've got to treat that cigar-smoking, cussing, old foreman as if he was Christ?" That is what it says, I told him; how can he know you are a Christian, if you are not an obedient servant?

"I must obey?"

"You could win him for Christ, if you do."

You can not go to your business desk or your bench without the Holy Spirit. He is still there. And He is waiting to help you to see how you behave. I know from experience how wonderful this can be, how men have been blessed at work, because of their faithfulness to the Lord.

A great theologian, who by his own admission was a liberal, and Dr. Mackay of Princeton Theological

Seminary, did not agree: the liberal believed the World Council must first be organized, and then God would help us to unity. Mackay said: "No! The unity must come from the Spirit, not from organization. You can't organize the Holy Ghost." These two always amused me with their arguments, though the liberal did not like me at all. And one day Dr. Mackay said to him: "If you knew what du Plessis was trying to do, you would invite him to your seminary."

"What good are these Pentecostals, anyway?" he retorted. "What do they have to offer?"

"Well," said Mackay, "why don't you go south of the border and find out? They're having a revival down in Central and South America."

The theologian accepted the challenge. "All right, I've come to my sabbatical year. I'll take it, and I promise you: I'm going to investigate the whole Pentecostal Movement."

So he and his wife went to Havana, Cuba (this was just before Castro) and checked in at the hotel. Then he asked the staff there: "Sunday's coming up; do you know of a church here where people are happy, and where there's a crowd, and where everybody seems to like to go?"

"Oh, yes. We go to one of those. The management gives us Sunday mornings off, and we do the rooms and the beds in the afternoons."

"Can my wife and I go with you?"

"Sure."

"When the taxi stopped, he looked out, and sure enough, it was a Pentecostal church. "That's what I thought it would be," he whispered to her, as they got out.

When they went in, the ushers sized him up as an important visitor, and promptly showed them to seats right up front. And things began to move. Young people came in, there was a huge grand piano over there, a brass band over here, and drums and so on, and in a few moments all were being played at once, as the congregation sang. I mean, they thundered!

The theologian leaned over to his wife and said: "You know what? I've heard Pentecostals don't go to honkey-tonks and night-clubs. Now I see why: they've got the band in the church! Well, it certainly draws the people! I wouldn't be surprised, if they dance!"

She said, "Well, turn around." And there was a grey-headed old lady, dancing up and down the aisle.

The singing stopped, and the pastor began to preach. After awhile, the liberal again leaned over and said to his wife, "I thought they could only shout hallelujah and talk in tongues. But this man's a theologian. He's preaching a marvelous message. It's wonderful!"

When the service was over, and they were leaving, he said to her, "I am agreeably surprised. I never knew what a Pentecostal meeting was like. What I have heard is altogether different from what I have seen here."

When they were outside, she asked, "Now what are you going to do?"

"Well," he said, "I've seen them at church. Tomorrow, I'm going to find out what they live like in public." And so, on Monday morning he got in a taxi and went to the biggest industrial plant in Havana. When he arrived, he asked to see the manager, and said, "Sir, I am on a research tour and would like to ask you some questions. You employ all kinds of people here?"

"Yes, anybody that wants work, comes here; we'll give them a job. If they don't know how to do it, we'll teach them."

"You employ all kinds of nationalities, too?"

"Yes."

"Do you employ Pentecostals?"

"Pentecostals? What nationality is that?"

"It's not a nation; it's a church."

"Oh," said the manager. "What are they?"

"I was in their church yesterday," the visitor explained. "They've got an orchestra, they sing, and they shout, and they clap hands."

"Ah!" exclaimed the manager. "We don't call them Pentecostals; we call them the Hallelujah People."

"The Hallelujah People?"

"Yes, because that's the only swear word they know."

"*Swear* word?"

"Yeah," the manager laughed, "one fellow hit his finger with a hammer, and he shouted, 'Hallelujah! Hallelujah! Hallelujah!' And afterwards, he claimed his finger was healed."

"As workers," the visitor persisted, "are they any good?"

"Oh," the manager said, nodding, "they are the best."

"Why?"

The manager looked at him. "Mister, I don't know who you are, or what you are, and I don't mean to be sacrilegious, but Jesus Christ is the best foreman we've got here. He's the foreman of all these Hallelujah People. They work under Him, and so you can trust them. They don't steal time; in fact, they don't steal anything. And they'll give you the best job. That's why any position of trust here belongs to a Pentecostal."

That testimony was so good that when this man came back to his seminary, he wanted all the students to become Pentecostal. Then he invited me to come and speak, and I marveled at the way the Lord changed this man's opinion. It was not me or a sermon or a book that persuaded him; it was the lives of those people down in Cuba. The way we live is so much more important than the way we talk. For we can talk straight and live crooked. That's why we must walk in the Spirit everywhere — at work and at home, as well as in church.

What about divine order in the church?

The church, of course, is the first place where we must walk in the Spirit. When I was about to become a young pastor in South Africa, there was a Dutch Reformed tradition which we followed to some extent. The Dutch Reformed Chruch would have Communion meetings once in three months, and I would see all their wagons coming from the farms. They would drive into the town camps and so on, and they would have meetings in preparation for the Communion. We always set aside Saturday night as preparation for Communion, so that we would not be guilty of eating and drinking damnation upon ourselves, as Paul had warned (I Corinthinas 11). Those Saturday evening meetings often turned into times of confession and reconciliation, so that when we went to the Lord's Table the following morning, it was with joyous, cleansed hearts.

I came to see that the process of repentance, reconciliation, and sharing the Lord's Supper together was an excellent way of keeping the Body of Christ united and in order. For by one Spirit were we baptized into one body, when we had the drink of Living Water, and were made to drink. When I became a pastor, I took that responsibility very seriously, for I considered it a great privilege to administer the eucharist.

Thinking about what Paul had said, regarding the necessity of discerning the Lord's Body, I realized that he was referring not to the host, but to the body of believers who would be partaking of the host. That was why we needed preparation for eating and drinking, if we were not truly united in the spirit.

In those early days, I saw another place where purity of heart was crucial: in praying for the sick. At that time, we believed that if the person doing the praying was guilty of anything, then the sick spirit could come out of the person being prayed for, and attack the one praying. We had a number of cases, where the sick were healed, but the people who prayed got sick. Why? Because they were not sheltered under the Blood. They had come out and were guilty of iniquity — sin that had not been forgiven and cleansed.

Later, when I was a pastor in Connecticut, there was a gravely ill sister from another church, who asked me to come and visit her. As she sat there in agony, she said, "Oh, Brother David, I'm glad you've come! Can you help me? I've had two doctors look at me. Fever is consuming me, and for two weeks my arms and legs have been covered with this running eczema."

I said, "Why did you call the doctors?"

"Well, I wanted medical advice — but they don't seem to know what's causing it."

"Are they elders of your church?" She shook her head,

and so did I. "Sister, the Bible says, when you're sick, call the elders of the church."

And she said to me, "Who are the elders of the church?"

"Well, your pastor is number one."

"Oh, I'm sorry, but I don't have any confidence in him at all."

I shrugged. "Now I know why you're sick."

"Why?"

"You took Communion from that pastor, didn't you?" She nodded. "That's where you got sick."

She looked at me, her eyes widening. "I did get sick in the church, right after I'd taken Communion! I had this attack and couldn't serve my family lunch that day. So here I am — and it won't go away."

I looked at her. "Do you realize what you've done? You ate and drank damnation upon yourself. And if you don't get this thing straightened out between you and your pastor, you might as well tell me what you want sung at your funeral, because 'some are weak and sick and some are dead'."

She says, "That's in the Bible?"

I nodded and read her the eleventh chapter of Paul's first letter to the believers in Corinth, where he spoke of the eucharist: "If you eat and drink, not discerning the Lord's body, then you eat and drink damnation upon yourself . . . ."

"I never heard that," she said softly, "and if I did read it, I didn't know what it meant."

"What did the pastor do that gave you such a bad opinion of him?" I asked her.

"I don't know what he did. I just heard a rumor. I don't know whether he really did anything at all."

"So you listened to some scandal?" I asked, and she nodded. "Well, sister, I don't know what else to tell you, but to get the thing straightened out, and the Lord will forgive you."

"Must I tell the pastor?"

"Doesn't he know?"

"Nobody knows, only me and the lady who told me — and now you."

I smiled. "Well, you've made a good confession to me; I'll tell you what: 'Why make a happy man sad?'"

"Thank you, brother David," she said, "I'm going to call the pastor and ask him to come over now and pray for me."

So that pastor and his wife came, and they prayed for her, and when they left, she said, "The fever is gone! They prayed for me, and now it's gone." She looked down at her arms. "Now, I feel dirty. Let me just go into the bathroom a moment."

When she returned, I saw a miracle. The running eczema on her limbs was washed off, and they were clear and perfectly healed.

As I got up to leave, I asked her, "What did you tell the Lord?"

"I promised Him that I would never again bear a grudge against any preacher, no matter who, especially when I went to Communion."

I sighed. "Dear sister, you must not have any quarrel with *anybody*, not just the pastor."

And she looked upward. "Dear Lord, help me, that I'll never bear a grudge against anybody at all," she paused, "and especially when I go to Communion."

Have you a word for pastors on this form of divine order?

Paul's warning applies on both sides of the Communion rail. I was in Portland, Oregon, and they invited me to a pastors' prayer meeting at the Baptist church at which I was speaking — at five o'clock in the morning. I didn't mind; I told them I would get up at any time, to pray with them. And I did. When we finished praying, I felt led to tell them the story of the woman in Connecticut, and one of the pastors burst out sobbing, "O Lord, have mercy on me!"

"What struck you?" I asked him.

"You said that if members are against their pastor and take Communion, they eat and drink damnation upon themselves." He wept. "What about the pastor who serves Communion to people that he hates?"

"I never thought of that," I admitted. "What's your experience?"

"Every time I serve Communion, there's a family there that won't go away. They come, and I hate them, even as I offer them the eucharist. And every time, I'm sick for a week afterwards. I didn't know why, until now. But thank God, He didn't let me suffer till I die!"

"What are you going to do?"

"Brother David, I'm going to humble myself; I'll make myself a *doormat*, if that's what it takes, but I'm going to be reconciled to that family!"

Three years later, I was back in Portland, and was invited to speak at this same Baptist minister's church. We passed a little white church, and I said, "Isn't that your church?"

"That *was* my church," he replied. "The new one is coming up, around the bend." And as we rounded the hill, there was a beautiful, big complex, with buildings, parking lots, and a big auditorium.

"*That's* your new church?"

He nodded. "You'll be speaking at the second meeting; we've already had a thousand people at the first."

I was delighted for him. "How in the world did this happen?"

"You remember, I told you I was determined to be reconciled? Well, I went to that family and asked their forgiveness, and we became very close. They're well-to-do and wanted to help, and we together, by the grace of God, have seen the work flourish."

And divine order for children?

I was thirty years old, married, and running a newspaper, when my father wrote me about my younger brother Justus, who was half my age: "I can no longer manage this boy. You and I had our difficulties and misunderstandings, but he is different than you; I cannot trust him at all. Will you take him over and handle him? I'm sure you'll know what to do."

So I wrote back, "Sure, Papa, let him come."

He came, and I welcomed him, and then sat down and said, "Now look: You are not under your father any more. He has given me full authority to be your guardian, and Anna and I will do our duty. But we expect you to be fair. We're not going to make things miserable for you. You come to church on Sunday mornings, Sunday evenings, and Wednesdays. Other than that, and going to school, you are free to come and go, as you choose. If you want to do sports or other school activities, that's fine. I want you to live in the world, and learn how the world lives. So far, I have had little to do with the world; our father would not have us take part in sports of any kind. If I spoke of sports for exercise, he would say, 'There's a garden to dig, and there's a door to fix, and so on. Tools are always ready'."

I had enjoyed no pleasures of the world, never played a game of any kind, although I often thought that if I ever did, tennis would be a game that I would like to play. But now, here came Justus, and here was I, telling him to play.

He was a little incredulous: "What will Papa say about it?"

"You have no concern about what Papa says, because you have to deal with me now, not him. You are free; you've been liberated from that life, and I understand what you've suffered. Papa thought I was backsliding, when I went to university, so he forbade me in the house and things like that. That's why I worked so hard at university: to prove him wrong."

So Justus went to school, and a little while later, he comes to me and says: "There is going to be a concert at school. Can I go?"

I nodded. "Neither you nor I are out of the world yet."

"You mean, you don't object?"

"Why should I?" And then I thought for a moment. "I suppose it's going to cost something — how much are the tickets?" He told me, and I gave him the price of two tickets.

"No," he said, looking at it, "it's only half this."

"Do you mean to tell me you're not going to take a girl?"

He looked at me, startled. "Um, she can pay her own ticket."

"No, you must learn to be a gentleman. You pay for her ticket." And then I gave him still more money.

Astonished, he asked, "What's this for?"

"You mean to tell me, you're going there and coming back home and not having any refreshments?" I frowned, then smiled. "That is to enjoy yourself a little."

He was speechless. Then he murmured, "Papa would never approve of this."

"Dear Justus," I quietly reminded him, "I am now in charge." And so, we won his confidence. All that we required of him was: "When you go out, tell us where you are going, and what time you'll be back, and keep your word. No all-night galavanting around." Anna added: "Justus, David is a pastor here. It's true he's the editor of the newspaper in this city, and manager of the printing press and all that, but he is still a pastor, a Pentecostal pastor. He still preaches on street corners, and the public here knows him. They are going to judge him by your behavior, so make sure that you never disgrace us."

He never did. And some time later, an English missionary from the Congo came to visit. He was an old friend and had thrilled me with his adventures, when I was a boy. Now he made a deep impression on Justus, who went to all his meetings. That was when he got his inspiration to become a missionary. After he had graduated, he married one of the girls in the church, and the two of them felt called to go and work among the Indians in Natal. Thus did he start out and become ordained in the district. At that time, I was District Secretary, and so I got them to ordain him and send him out to Durban, in Natal.

That was Indian country (India Indians), and to this

day, when Justus meets an Indian, he can still chat away
in Hindu. He made many friends quickly, and before
long the Indians asked him to be their representative to
the government. "I'll have to pray about that," he told
them. "I don't know whether the Lord wants me getting
mixed up in politics."

A week later, the government sent two fellows to him,
to ask him to be the government's representative to the
Indians. It was a bit of a dilemma, and so he called me
and asked, "What do I do now?"

I said, "They've ruined your future as a missionary, for
if you don't go with the Indians, they won't trust you ever
again. yet if you don't go with the government, they
won't trust you, either." I thought for a moment. "There
is only one way out: You've got to get out of there entirely
— in other words, resign."

It grieved him, for he had grown to love those people,
but he could see the wisdom in my suggestion, and he
resigned. And our friendship, based on mutual trust, continued to grow. All because I had insisted from the outset
that he accept the divine order he found in our home,
and because at the same time I demonstrated a modicum
of hard-earned compassion.

Finally, what about divine order in the congregation?

A few years ago, at the suggestion of Bishop Cannon,
the Methodist representative at the Vatican Council, I
was invited to come and minister to a thousand
Methodist ministers. "What do you want me to tell
them?" I asked.

"Tell them what the Spirit is saying to the Church in this day."

"Oh, that would be a privilege! But tell me: these thousand ministers — you didn't mention their wives. They will be with them, won't they?"

"Oh, no," he said, surprised that I would even ask. "We never invite the women."

"Then don't invite me. I'm sick and tired of talking to half a man!" — or half a woman, for that matter, which is why I never accept a Full Gospel Businessmen's speaking invitation, unless they also invite Women Aglow. I was with Demos Shakarian, when the Full Gospel Businessmen first got started, and when he wouldn't include women, I encouraged the women in Seattle to establish their own society. That was how Women Aglow got started, and I was their first preacher. And now, I never accept *their* invitation, unless they invite the Full Gospel Businessmen. I always get the two together.

And now I've gone further than that: If a minister comes to me, and wants to consult me on church matters, I say, "Only if your wife comes with you, for she must be with you in it."

One woman pleaded with Anna to get me just to speak to her for a few minutes, and Anna pleaded with me, and I agreed. When she arrived, the first thing I asked her was: "Are you married?"

"Yes."

"Where's your husband?"

"Oh, he's busy."

"Doing what?"

"He's working at the church."

"You mean to tell me, he's a minister?"

She nodded. "He's a Baptist minister."

"Then, lady, this is the end of our conversation."

"What! Why?"

"Because I will not listen to you, unless your husband is present."

"But —"

"No buts. I'll pray with you now, and that's the end. Now give me your hand," and I took it and prayed, "Lord, you know this sister's problem, and I've perhaps made it more difficult. But I ask you to let her here and now decide that she will be submissive to her husband. And Lord, help her to win him."

She went to his office at the church, I learned later, and as soon as she came in, he said, "What did that Pentecostal say?"

"He wouldn't talk to me."

"What do you mean?"

"He asked me if I was married, and when I told him I was, he wondered where you were. When I told him that you were a pastor and working at the church, he said, 'Then I've got *nothing* to say. I don't talk to preacher's wives without the preacher present."

He said, "This Pentecostal I must meet!"

So they came, and it turned out that their problem was that she wanted the Baptism, and he was afraid of it. I explained it to them, and the Lord baptized them both in the Holy Spirit together. Now they were united as never before — a husband-and-wife team, ready to present (and represent) the fullness of God.

6

GROWING UP

The author's life has been well chronicled in the excellent autobiography, A Man Called Mr. Pentecost, *which he wrote with Bob Slosser, in 1977. But with the gathering of years, fresh insights give familiar incidents new meaning. In this chapter, the author shares his latest thinking on some of the physical — and spiritual — growing lessons he learned in the early days in South Africa.*

"Honor your father and mother . . . that it may be well with you and you may live long on the earth" (Ephesians 6:2). Not only is that the first commandment with a promise attached, it is a promise that works. When friends say, "David, you've really lived beyond the measure of threescore and ten," I tell them, "Yes, because I honored my father and mother. That's why I live on."

My father did the same, and lived till he was 84. But at 80, he wrote to me: "You remember how often I told you with a smile that I intend to live 120 years? Well, I'm tired now, and I find that I'm not much use. This is quite long enough to live; I'm ready to go home." And he

added that he wished the Lord to take him home on
Ascension Day.

On that day, four years later, I was at Kennedy Airport
in New York, on my way to Jerusalem for a conference,
and I called Anna. "I've got bad news for you," she said.

"What's the matter?"

"There's a cable here: Your father passed away this
morning."

I shook my head. "Dear old Dad. He wanted to go
home on Ascension Day, because Jesus went on that day.
In fact, he was so sure of it that he once wrote me,
'David, if I'm sick, don't worry, I won't die. I'm not
going to be put out of this old house by a sick devil.'"

Later, at the conference, I had a chance to talk with a
pastor friend of my father's. "I believe you were with my
dad, when he passed away."

"Yes, I came by to pick up some things, and he was
sitting out there, in the shade of the grapevine. 'Grandpa,'
I called, 'I've come to fetch my camp equipment.'

" 'Well,' he said, 'it's in the garage; you know where it
is. But Pastor, do you know I've asked the Lord to take
me home today?' "

"In that case, Grandpa," said the pastor, "have you
still got some of that unfermented wine that you make
from your grapes?"

"One gallon."

"Before you go, can you let me have it?"

Grandpa got up, fetched the gallon of wine, and as the
pastor paid for it, he told him, "Now brother, you go and
get your equipment; the garage is open. I'm a little tired;
I'll just sit down."

As the pastor walked towards the garage, he heard
Grandpa say, "Hallelujah!" But he sounded a bit strange,

so the pastor turned back and saw him slumped over in the chair.

"I ran to him, lifted him up, and your mother came out of the house, and I said, 'Grandma, Grandpa's fainted.' Grandma came along slowly, all smiles, and when she got there, she took his pulse and said, 'He hasn't fainted; he's gone.' "

The pastor shook his head at the recollection and commented on how easily my mother seemed to be taking it. "Pastor, he said goodbye to me at breakfast this morning. He told me that the Lord might not give him a chance to come in the house and say goodbye."

Fortunately, this pastor had his oldest daughter in the car, and she happened to be head nurse at the Johannesburg Hospital — a brilliant girl with the equivalent of a doctor's degree. She came over and took my Dad's pulse and said, "He's gone, for sure, and as far as I can tell, without any suffering. He just gave up the ghost."

She called a doctor friend who came over and waived the need for a post-mortem. So the Lord undertook for everything, and that was how my old Dad went home.

Were you and your father always close?

When I was young, my father was very hard on me, and I never knew why. When I informed him of my decision to go to university, he was extremely upset; he was convinced that I would not last. One day years later, my mother said to me, "I'd better tell you the truth: When you and your father went to Johannesburg for the conference, there was an old brother there who claimed to be a prophet. When your father asked him: 'What has the Lord showed you about my two oldest boys?' he replied, 'Oh, ya, I have figured them out: That fair-haired one (me) is no use; you can't take his word. He'll never be good for anything. But that black-haired one (my younger brother), he is the man! A real prince!' When he came home, he told me that he was going to knock it into you, because there was no other way."

So, finally, I understood, but I still found it strange that my father, a wise man, would put such stock in the so-called 'prophecy' of such a man — who later was imprisoned for raping a girl.

What sort of influence did your father have on your life?

For one thing, in dress he was a real gentleman. He had his overalls on for his work, but when he came home, he always took them off, or sometimes he would leave them at work, when he went to visit. And so, to this day, it is my way. I am more comfortable in a jacket and tie than anything else, and especially when I am visiting. And it continues in the family: my son has his own company, and he is always ready to go and visit the people who he works for. But he does not go in dirty clothes. As he is about his body, so he is in spirit.

What was the first thing that attracted you to Life in the Spirit?

Miracles, of course — when I was a young lad, that was all I wanted to do. I said: "Lord, I want to do miracles like the Africans. They do miracles." I had read through the Bible, and I thought I knew why: the Africans were too dumb to know what was impossible.

They never thought; they never argued about impossibilities. They just believed that with God, all things were possible. And I saw them do miracles. But it was not until I accompanied Wigglesworth, as his interpreter, that I saw the Lord dispense miracles of healing "wholesale," so to speak.

You often refer to Wigglesworth — who was he?

Smith Wigglesworth was a visiting English evangelist who had one peculiarity: totally unlearned, he was to become known worldwide for starting Pentecost in countries where others had not succeeded at all. He was invited, for instance, to New Zealand and to Australia and brought tremendous blessing. But he never had one day of schooling. At eight, he began to work with his father in tinsmithing. Donald Gee then told me about him and suggested that he would be a very good evangelist to get to come to South Africa, because he was so simple in his approach, and he did not forget to tell them that he could read only the Bible. He couldn't read road signs or anything.

The Lord, he said, helped him to read the Bible, and what an encouragement that was to the black people — here was a white brother that the Lord was using mightily and who had no education. Many blacks used to think that to be a Christian, you had to be educated. One missionary from Sweden had worked in Africa for seven years and had not baptized a single convert. Finally, he said that it was time for him to go home. In his farewell to them, he said, "My heart is aching. I love you, but not one convert have I baptized."

They said to him, "Well, we thought we ought to wait till you told us that we were suitable for baptism. We didn't know that we were supposed to ask you to baptize us, because we're uneducated, unlearned."

"Oh, no!" he laughed, "I've been waiting for *you* to tell *me* you wanted to be baptized." But here was a clear picture of a missionary who had inadvertantly given the impression they must be educated, because he encouraged them to read. Before he left, they flocked to the meetings and wanted to be baptized. And so, he had the privilege of baptizing nearly a thousand people and then go home and tell everyone that he had reaped the harvest in the end, before he departed.

Wigglesworth was not only an evangelist, but a man with a prophetic ministry. I was his interpreter and accompanied him most places. He said to me, "You're the first man who has interpreted for me without asking me what I've said, or what I meant."

"I follow the train of your thoughts," I said. "I know what you mean, even when you concoct words that you can't find in a dictionary."

I had great confidence in him, because I witnessed so many marvelous, instantaneous miracles in his meetings. I remember in particular one Sunday morning in 1936, just before my 31st birthday, in a church where he stood up after we had been singing, and he said, "Now the Lord has laid a special message on my heart this morning, but I don't want people to suffer while I'm preaching, and I can't have a healing line on a Sunday morning — there's not time. So, let us first have retail healing."

Retail healing? Goodness me, I'd never heard of that expression before. What was retail healing? Was it scriptural? He said, "Anybody here who's ill this morning, suffering pain? You know that if you're healed, the pain will leave you, and you'll be free at once; you could tell immediately whether you're healed or not. But if you don't get healed, then you're going to suffer all during the meeting."

A man and a woman stood up, and in his Yorkshire way of talking, Wigglesworth said, "What's up with you?" They told him the pain, and he said to the woman: "I command you to be healed!" Then he made her bend and stretch, and the lady began to laugh. When she did, Wigglesworth said, "Tell us, are you healed?"

"*Oh yes!* No pain, no pain! I'm healed!"

"Well, praise the Lord! You may sit down." He turned to the man. "Now, what's up with you?" The man had the same kind of arthritis. Wigglesworth said: "In Jesus' name, be healed!" He paused, then added, "Now do what you think you cannot do. Do what you haven't been able to do." The man began to throw himself around, and there was a great shout in the camp.

"Well," said Wigglesworth, "there you are! Two retail healings, and you know, of course, what you can get retail, you can always get wholesale. Now, let's have wholesale. Everybody in this meeting who's sick, from your head to your toes, anything at all wrong with you, stand up." And a whole crowd got to their feet. He said, "In Jesus' name, I command you *all* to be healed! Now sit down!"

Afterwards, people would come to me and say that in other services, he would pray for them, shake them, hold their hands, and they wouldn't get healed. "Why, this morning, in this wholesale business, did we get healed?"

I said, "I'll tell you why: when he prayed for you and

was going to lay hands on you, you wanted Wiggles-worth to heal you. You had the foolish idea that he had the gift to heal. There is no such gift in the Bible. There are gifts *of* healing, and the only people who receive a gift of healing are those who are sick. When Wiggles-worth came with wholesale healing, you knew he wasn't going to lay hands on you. You had to look to Jesus to heal you. And He did! Wigglesworth has taught you a lesson: don't believe that anybody has the gift *to* heal."

As for prophecy, brother Wigglesworth had a strong word from the Lord for me: *If David keeps faithful, I will bless him, and if I bless him, he must keep humble about it. If he can keep faithful and humble to the end of his life, he will see things that nobody has ever seen or heard or known were possible.* Many of the things that Wigglesworth told me have come true or happened literally the way he said they would. And when he prophesied that I would go forth for the Lord, he did say I would go to "*all* the Christian churches, and must always reach for the top leaders, and work down."

But at first, I rejected his words. "I can't listen to a prophet. New Testament prophecy is only for three things: edification, exhortation and comfort, and I don't think I need any of that. So," I concluded, "I cannot listen to what you say."

He said, "I didn't give you any instruction. I gave you a warning, don't you remember? I said that the Lord told me to warn you that He was going to use you, and that the Holy Spirit would use you."

"Oh, I see."

"I didn't tell you what you've got to do; I told you what the Lord was *going* to do."

"Well, that's true, too. In the Acts of the Apostles, the

Lord told them what He was going to do. 'You shall receive power after the Holy Ghost has come upon you.' " And so I was able to accept his words for me — and have been grateful ever since. And now, I am just looking to see what the end will be, because he did not live to see the end; in fact, he said he would be gone to glory, before I even started with the new ministry.

Who else was a major influence on your early life in the spirit?

What Pope John was to the Charismatic movement in the Catholic Church, Andrew Murray was to the Pentecostal revival in South Africa, and the man whom I worked under as president of the movement, Peter Louis le Roux was Andrew Murray's first missionary student. He was a school teacher, whom Andrew Murray took into his family, trained, educated in theology and in missions, and finally sent to Zululand, to be a missionary.

Le Roux became the president of the Movement, and I worked with him for sixteen years. In all that time, I never heard him use a wrong word or say anything terrible. He was a saint, if ever there was one — the sweetest, most perfect man I ever knew.

Certainly in the Movement, he was a steadying influence; if people got out of order, he would beautifully calm them down and let them enjoy the blessing of the Lord, without getting fanatical about it, or going overboard on demonstration. When he retired — in South Africa, by introducing a financial system of tithing, I had helped to make retirement at 65 possible, never dreaming that it would soon become mandatory (was I glad to be out of there, before I turned 65!) — I missed him very much. The man who replaced him as president was my junior, and in terms of experience, a novice. But it was generally believed that I would be more valuable to the Movement as its secretary than as its president; indeed, it was felt that the Movement could not really function with anyone else. So, while I did not get the promotion that many thought I should have had, I was content; I knew the Lord was in it, for He had already indicated that He had other plans for me. . . .

One day, I asked brother Le Roux: "How old were you, when you got victory over your thoughts? Because I'm still having trouble with mine."

"Oh," he laughed, "I'm not that old yet."

"You mean, you still have trouble?"

"Well, I'm not troubled with *young* man's thoughts any more; now I've got *old* man's thoughts to worry about."

"Really? It keeps on?"

He nodded. "This is the enemy, shooting his fiery darts into your mind," and smiling at my unspoken question, he added, "the Scripture says, 'Quench with the shield of faith,' so either do that, or simply let the darts go in one ear and out the other, and forget them." (Years later, I would hear of some old friends who would answer that question with a Chinese proverb: Just because a bird circles around your head, you don't have to let it make a nest in your hair.)

I pressed Le Roux; I had to know exactly what he did. "Well," he chuckled, "I must admit that sometimes I feel like Luther did, the day he grew so vexed at the devil that he flung his inkwell at him. But you really can let those thoughts go in one ear and out the other. Next time, try it." I did, and it worked, and I came to see that it was not what went in or out of a man's head that mattered; but as a man thought in his *heart*, so was he. And the Lord judges us not by our head, but by our hearts.

7

WALKING IN
THE WAY

One of the first things a new Christian must learn is
no longer to depend totally on the logic and reason of
one's mind, but to listen inwardly for the still, small
voice of the Holy Spirit. With practice, one comes to
know one's Shepherd's voice, and to trust it, even
when what that voice is saying, or the course it is
suggesting, seems illogical or unreasonable. And as
one gets used to listening — and heeding — one
develops a certain inner peace . . . .

I have a philosophy, which I learned in Germany, at
the first Ecumenical Conference. There, I came across a
German saying, which I translated into: "Happy is the
man who can endure, what he cannot cure." So I never
get worried. If anything goes wrong, and it is not my
fault, and there is nothing I can do to help, I just endure
it and wait to see what will happen.

My wife Anna and I were leaving on a plane trip from the
San Francisco airport, and just when we expected the

boarding to be announced, they said, "There'll be an hour and a half delay. They've found something wrong with the plane."

Anna said, "Why didn't they tell us before we left the house?"

"My dear, they just found out there's something wrong."

"Well, what are we going to do?"

"I'm going to sleep. There's a nice chair here."

"You can sleep?"

"Yes. Why worry? There's nothing I can do to help them fix the plane," and I settled into the chair. "Wake me up when they call," I murmured, closing my eyes.

Living by and in the Holy Spirit has become a way of life for the author, and the older he grows, the more clear everything becomes. Here, he recalls his first meeting with the late, world-renowned theologian, Karl Barth.

The most perfect church in the New Testament was Ephesus, and the letter Paul wrote to that church is very rich in teaching, and wonderfully deep. But I notice how concerned he is that "I would not have you ignorant." I met that word again during my first encounter with Professor Karl Barth. He had urged his son Marcus to get in touch with me, for he had heard what I was doing, and what I was teaching, and he wanted to learn from me about the Holy Spirit.

I was living in Basel then, but when I was there he was in Germany, and when he was in Switzerland, I was in America, so it was some time, before we finally met. When we finally did, he exclaimed, "This is wonderful! Tell me all about the Holy Spirit, as you know Him."

And I said, "But Professor, you are such a researching theologian; you must have reached some conclusions from your teaching, or from your studies. If I tell you anything that you already know, please tell me; don't let me waste your time and my time."

"You think I'm a fundamentalist," he responded, as if offended.

I shook my head. "That depends on what you mean by a fundamentalist — what *is* a fundamentalist?"

"Don't you know? A fundamentalist is somebody who knows some Scripture and thinks he has arrived. If you don't agree with him, you're lost. But if you have more than he's got, you've gone astray." He smiled. "Never worry about them, because they don't want to go anywhere. They think they've arrived."

"Well," I said, laughing, "you haven't arrived then?"

"No, thank God, no!"

"Don't you ever expect to arrive?"

"Heaven forbid!"

"Why not?" I persisted.

"Don't you know? Jesus Christ said, 'I am the way' — and that is a way without a terminal. You'll never arrive. And if you go on in this way, the truth shall make you free. But you must be walking in the way. As you travel, you can look at a map and say, 'Well, I see the way there,' but once you start traveling, you'll find out there are some things that you'll learn that are not on the map."

"And then, that makes you free from what?"

"It liberates you from ignorance." Oh, dear, I thought; I hope this is not going to be Liberation Theology.

"Liberates you from ignorance?"

"The great tragedy in Christianity is that so many are *ignorant*. They sing 'Jesus loves me, this I know' — but they don't *know* it. They have no idea of what God can

do, will do, for them and through them. They suffer
from such ignorance that they really cannot make a contribution towards the renewal of the whole world.
Consequently, ignorance is the greatest bondage in
Christianity. And if you are ignorant of what God can
and will do, how can you ever enjoy the abundant life?
You are bound by ignorance, and you're like a man who
is handcuffed and tries to swim. You'll surely drown."
He held up his hands. "Take me, for instance: I know my
ignorance about the things of the Spirit, as I now find
that things are happening in the world that, I must
admit, are true to Scripture, but are not true to the traditions of the Church."

As we were talking, every now and then he would say,
"Oh, that is so beautiful! Now that is simply the truth!
But theologians say it this way, or theologically speaking,
you must first demonstrate this."

"Professor," I replied, "you've told me what a fundamentalist is. Now tell me what theology is."

"Don't let that bother you," he laughed. "It is merely
the art of making simple things confusing."

That helped me no end. And it was then that I began
to realize that the Lord had given me a ministry of making confusing things simple again.

Is the truth always so simple?

Karl Barth's words would come back to me, sooner
than I expected. Speaking in Greenwich to a gathering of
leading theologians, I found that confusing was indeed
the word for the questions they were asking me. But to
my surprise, when I told them what we Pentecostals
believed, I heard some of them murmur, "How pro-

found!" I had to smile at that; I was making it so simple that a kindergartener could understand it. That was when it really struck me that the truth was not so mysterious and so difficult that we could not grasp it — if we kept it simple.

What does "walking in love" mean?

In writing to the Ephesians, the Apostle Paul says in the second chapter: "And you hath he quickened who were dead in trespasses and sins, wherein (time past) ye walked according to the course of this world, according to the prince of the power of the air, the spirit that now worketh in the children of disobedience." What does he mean by walk? He just means *live* — you live this way. This is the way you walk every day.

Further on, we come to verse 10: "For we are his workmanship, created in Christ Jesus unto good works which God hath ordained before that we should walk in them." That's a new walk — a new way of living. And if Jesus is the Way, that way is made to walk in. You must walk this way.

Paul goes on, and in the fifth chapter says: "Be ye, therefore, followers of God, as dear children, and walk in love, as Christ has loved us and has given Himself for an offering and a sacrifice to God for a sweet smelling savor."

And walking in the light?

"Walk as children of light," we are commanded, for as Jesus said, "You are the light of the world."

I have had evangelicals ask me: "David, don't you know those people are in darkness?"

"That's funny, I've never seen it."

"You don't see the darkness?"

"No, where I go, it's always light. I have light, and darkness cannot put out my light. Darkness cannot even put out a little candle." A scientist was once asked how far a candle could be seen in total darkness. His answer: fifty miles. When I read that, I exclaimed, "Dear Lord, thank you that I can walk through darkness, because then they can see me. But if I'm where all the shining lights already are, what's the good of that? One more candle doesn't show up very much."

We are children of light, intended to walk in the light. "For the fruit of the Spirit is all goodness and righteousness and truth, proving what is acceptable unto the Lord" (Ephesians 5:10). This is the light; this is the way we've got to walk.

Can we always be in the Spirit?

Of course! Jesus was baptized in the Spirit, and John saw the Spirit descend upon Him and *"remain on Him."* Some churches, when they ask me to speak, have a way of calling me into the vestry and saying: "Let's lay hands on brother David, and ask the Lord to give him an anointing."

"No, you don't," I reply. "I don't need an anointing. I have been under the anointing since 1918, when Jesus baptized me in the Holy Spirit." Nor will I sing such silly songs as, "Spirit of the Living God, fall afresh upon me." Where has He gone?

The other song that I am accused of having ruined is, "Fill My Cup, Lord." Do you know if you pray that, you make Jesus a liar? He said: "One drink, and you'll never thirst again."

How about others giving you the benefit of their guidance?

As a rule, I would prefer that they didn't. But every good rule has its exception, and my wife Anna is mine. After so many years together, she knows me well enough to know where it might be me and not the Spirit, and I know her well enough to value her opinion. In the unions that God joins together, He gives us the mates we need, though sometimes we are reluctant to admit it.

But even Anna is not infallible. Listening to me preach — and she's a good listener — she sometimes says, "I get butterflies in my stomach when you say things. Now, why do you say such silly things, or such dangerous things?" One day I said something that so upset her, she thought, "What a terrible thing for David to say! I must warn him never to say it again!" And as soon as I finished, she rushed through the crowd, to get to me before I got too busy with people coming up. But an old lady grabbed her arm and held her, saying, "Ah, that husband of yours, he is a marvel! He gave me today just the words I needed, when he said — " and she repeated the very thing that Anna was hurrying to rebuke me for.

She said to me afterwards, "I just turned around and said, 'Dear Lord, help me that I won't become a hindrance to David.' I didn't think that there was anybody alive that needed a word like that!"

So, for the most part, I make sure that what I do, or what I say, is not because I have heard something from someone. That is why I do not want people to tell me what they have discerned. When they try, I tell them, "Now look, you must leave me alone and let the Holy Spirit tell me. If you give me information now, then I might have difficulty, because it is hard for me to know whether what I'm sensing is from my self, or from the Spirit."

A good example of this occurred when an old pastor called me. I had not met him, but he had my telephone number, and he called and asked, "Where are you going next Sunday?"

"I'm not going anywhere; I have to be in Pittsburgh the following week."

"Oh, good! That's exactly what I'd hoped! Could you possibly go to Pittsburgh two days early, so that you can preach for my son on Sunday? He has a church there, and he's a good boy, but he's having difficulties and the whole church needs encouragement. I know you can help him, and I'm sure he'll treat you well."

Listening to this father's plea, I felt that I should go. "All right, sir, will you let your son know that you've contacted me?"

"Yes."

"Then I will call him, as soon as I know my time of arrival."

When the young pastor met me, it was late in the evening, and so he said, "I think the best thing is to get you to bed for a good night's sleep, so that you'll be fresh in the morning." That was about the extent of our conversation, and I didn't ask him anything.

I awoke the next morning, thinking about what his father had told me about these people needing encouragement. Well, I had just the message for their edification, something that would really help them. But as I prayed, I realized that that was not the message which the Lord would have me bring. *He* wanted me to preach to them on "Walking in the Spirit." Right away, I sensed that this was going to be a rough assignment.

Anyway, I went and preached on how you walk in the Spirit, and at times the teaching was so hard, you could cut the tension in the congregation with a knife. Even as I preached, I thought, "Dear Lord, there must be real trouble in this church, because I am repeatedly touching on points that I feel are hitting the nail on the head, so strong is the reaction." Nevertheless, on I went, and the Spirit brought to mind things I had forgotten for years — stories of my early years in South Africa, and some of the trials and troubles I had gone through.

After the meeting, as we went for refreshment, the young pastor privately asked me: "Whatever possessed you to preach that sermon?"

I shrugged. "I had a very nice message of encouragement in mind, but the Lord said, *That is a good sermon, but it is not the message for this church.*"

The young pastor looked out the window. "If you don't come back this evening and tell them that I never told you anything in advance, they are going to believe that I poured out my heart to you about each one of them. Because as you preached, you didn't know it, but you started with the problems of the people in the first pew and then dealt with those in the second pew, and so on, pew by pew, exposing everybody, right to the back of the church." He shook his head at the recollection. "And *why* did you have to tell that story about a member of your church in South Africa that you caught smoking?"

I held up my hands. "Would you believe, I haven't thought of that in thirty years?"

"Well, when you said that, a man in our congregation glared at me, as if to say: 'You told him that!' Because I happened upon him in the A&P yesterday, the last place he ever expected to see me. I wheeled my cart around the corner, and there he was with a cigarette in his hand." He looked out the window again. "And there are other things . . ."

His voice trailed off, and I asked him gently, "And did I speak to their pastor, too?"

He nodded. "The funny thing is, when it pertained to me, you turned around and looked right at me."

"Well — what did I say?"

He pointed to the view out the window. "You see that hill there? That mountain? My father and I stood on top of that hill. There was nobody in sight, let alone within earshot, and there we talked about something . . . I'm going to talk to my father, because I'm sure he must have told you something."

"No," I replied emphatically, "I've never met your father."

"But he sent you here."

"Yes, by telephone. And the sum total of what he told me was that you were a good boy, but you were having difficulty here in the church."

He turned and looked at me — and apparently deciding that I was telling the truth, he smiled. "Well, you have certainly opened up the whole thing. And I got a shock, because the very words which I confided to my dad, you repeated. I was certain he had told you."

"No," I said again, "but the Holy Spirit knows you even better than your father."

"Then you know nothing about me?"

"Absolutely nothing."

He relaxed and smiled. "Now I feel better."

That was how I came to realize that, if I am yielded to the Spirit, and have no knowledge of anybody or anything before me, then I speak with great liberty.

8

LIVING BY FAITH

Living with no visible means of support, dependent entirely upon the mercy of God, is one of the most difficult vocations of the modern era. The author has been living that way for most of his adult life, often with surprising results, and always with his faith being stretched even further.

"Wherefore be ye not unwise but understanding what the will of God is" (Ephesians 5:17). That is so important: understanding what the will of God is. That does not mean that we will *know* the will of God, but we will understand why certain things happen. Then we can believe that all things — not just all blessings, but all things — will work together for good to them that love the Lord.

Some things I know of have worked together for good that did not look so pleasant, when they happened. Anna and I sometimes talk about our past, and what we would like to have changed. But we would never change the things that were suffering to go through, because from them came the greatest blessings and the greatest miracles.

Part of it was that we had to come to the place where we would be considered very poor, simply because we had no money. (I do not think people are rich, just because they have money; I know a lot of people who have money and are terribly poor.) We were poor, and yet it was a form of discipline that helped us to learn to trust Him.

One morning, as I left the house for work, Anna said to me, "You can come home for lunch, but there is nothing to eat."

"Nothing to eat?"

"No. We've eaten the last of the bread. There is nothing to put on the table at all."

I shook my head. "I'm afraid I'm not coming alone; there are other fellows to come home with me. Don't worry," I said, going out the door, "the Lord will provide."

My, it smelled good, when we opened the door and came in! And here was beautiful fish and potatoes and everything! "Where did this come from?" I whispered.

"You know the neighbor next door? The one who has never talked to me? This morning I was in my garden, and she was in her garden, and she came to the fence and said, 'Mrs. du Plessis, we have not spoken to each other, but my husband and one of my sons went out fishing, and they caught so much fish that I've got no room for it. Would you care to enjoy some?' and she handed me fish after fish over the fence. And a lady down the street, where she got the idea I don't know, but she sent me some potatoes." And so the Lord had undertaken for us, and we had a lovely lunch!

It turned out that that lady down the street had heard from friends that we were living by faith, and so, ever after that, whenever a car stopped in front of the house, she quickly sent all kinds of things there, for fear that we might not have something to treat our visitors with.

The Lord took care of us in so many ways. It may have looked like we were beggars, but I don't think children of God are beggars; they have got a rich father. One of the great multi-millionaires of South Africa used to stay at the Carlton Hotel, and when he left, he would tip the porter one pound. One day, the porter said to him: "Sir, when your son stays here, he always gives us five pounds, but you give us only a pound."

"Well," he said, "my son has a very rich father; I don't." It all depends on who your father is.

Speaking of fathers, didn't yours start you living by faith?

My father was a carpenter and a builder, and when he went to work for the missionaries, that had to be a faith-life. And so I learned early to tithe. My parents were very faithful in tithing, and when my mother inherited some money, they gave the whole lot to the church. They said, "The Lord can bless us for the future; that money couldn't bless us forever, like He can. It won't last." So they gave it away.

A few years later, when I was sixteen, my father gave *me* away, so to speak. There was a missionary meeting, and the missionary was asking for donkeys to work in the northern province. Horses didn't do very well up there; they died of sickness. But donkeys would live anywhere. And so he got donkeys — two with a cart, and another one besides. Then my father stood up. "I have a donkey I will give to the Lord," and I wondered what on earth he was talking about; we had no donkey. Just then he said, "David, come up here." I did, and he took me by the ear and said, "This is the donkey, my oldest son. Before he was born, his mother and I prayed that the Lord would bless him, and we dedicated his life to the ministry. We didn't expect the Lord to call him so soon," he went on, "but he's saved and baptized in the Spirit, and he's ready; he's applied for a position here in headquarters, as an apprentice in the print shop."

That was how David, the donkey, first got interested in publishing and printing. We printed the church newspaper on a press that was 70 years old. I got no salary; all they gave me was room and board in a widow's house. And there I learned to live by faith.

One Sunday morning, I looked in my drawer for my white shirt to wear to church, and it wasn't there! I went to the landlady and said, "Sister, there was a white shirt in the wash."

"Oh," she said, "I'm sorry, it came out all torn; there was nothing I could do to save it. But don't you have another?" I shook my head. "Well, then, you'd better stay in bed."

I went back to my room and lay on the bed, and I said, "Lord, I want to work for you, but this is something I don't understand. What am I to do? I don't want to miss the meeting this morning."

So, I began to think: suppose the Lord would do a miracle and put a shirt in my suitcase? I got up and opened it, and lo and behold — no shirt. Only a large linen handkerchief that my mother had sent with me. Feeling very sorry for myself, I stared at that big, good-for-nothing handkerchief, and then a curious thought came to me: in those days, we wore separate collars with our dress shirts . . . and with a suit, a vest and tie, of course . . . you know, it just might work! I took the linen handkerchief and made a small hole in it, for the collar button, put the collar in place with button and stud, and with a vest and tie on, at a casual glance one could not easily tell that I did not have a shirt on.

Thanking God for the inspiration, and rejoicing that Old Slewfoot could not keep me from church, I hurried to the service and slipped into the last pew. With nothing on my back and no sleeves, let alone cuffs, I felt distinctly naked, but at least I was in position to exit swiftly, as soon as the meeting was over. When the benediction was spoken, and I was about to turn for the door, an usher came up and took my arm, saying: "Somebody gave me this, and said I must give it to you. The Lord told them to give you this," and he thrust a wadded up piece of paper into my hand.

I mumbled thanks, stuffed it in my pocket, and left, figuring it was a piece of candy. When I was far enough away from the church, I paused and opened it — and gasped: it was a ten-shilling note! Hallelujah, my first ministry offering! I walked the rest of the way home on cloud nine. "Devil, you couldn't keep me in bed today! I made it to church, and look: the Lord gives me money to buy a new shirt! And now I know, if I go on and never stop, just because I haven't got everything I need, He will provide for my needs, as I go." It was a lesson to last a lifetime. And I learned another thing: you are only tested once, and if you pass that test, you are never tested in that direction again.

And later, when you were a successful publisher?

I had been transferred to the Orange Free State, to a little town called Bethlehem, where in addition to pastoring, I had taken over the management of a nearly-defunct printing press which was also turning out a weekly newspaper. When I took over, it was being published in English, in an Afrikaans area, and had a circulation of perhaps 500. The first thing I did was make it bilingual, and soon the circulation was up to 1,500 and then 2,000. In six months, we had caught up and paid all the outstanding debts. We also printed the national Pentecostal magazine, of which I was the editor.

By the grace of God and endless amounts of hard work, we were able to turn that operation around and make it profitable. In fact, despite being in the depths of the Depression, it became so successful, that soon Anna and I had another difficult decision to make. It came as a result of a speech I made at the dedication of the new town hall, on behalf of the Chamber of Commerce.

The speech went over so well, that the board of directors of the printing business — men who were good friends but not Pentecostals — wanted me to quit the ministry and give my undivided attention to business. They also wanted me to run for the school board and then the town council. To hear them talk, there was literally no limit to how far I might rise — first locally, then regionally and nationally. "This isn't right," they said, "that you speak for the businessmen one day, and then speak for the churches. You must resign from the church. We will give you a better salary, or a commission on all the work you do."

As I always do, I asked my wife what she thought. "Look, we can have a car! They'll buy a new car for the company." I must confess, I was taken with the prospect.

Anna wasn't. "You know your father and mother had prayed for their first-born to be a son, so they could train him and give him to the Lord. And now you want to go not into the spiritual realm . . . I can see how I might have a husband who's very popular, and have a big life, but I'm afraid I couldn't trust him. Because if he cannot be faithful to God, how can I trust that he'll be faithful to me?"

I was not convinced, but at the next directors' meeting, things suddenly came to a head. When I told them that the bank had refused to grant us an overdraft for the additional working capital we needed, one feisty old man said, "Tell them to go to hell!"

I was shocked, not at the outburst, but at the clarity of the choice which it laid before me. "Mr. Van der Poel," I said, after a moment, "I am trying to get people to go to heaven."

"Yes, yes, I know; that's not your language. I mean, tell them to get out of the way." So we changed banks, and I learned something about how rich people handled money. I took care of everything, and the directors were well pleased with my performance, and I began to enjoy the feeling of power that went with it.

But I was also growing increasingly uneasy in my spirit. This was not what God intended. So finally, I went to Anna. "What would you say, if I resigned from the paper and we ask the brethren in Johannesburg headquarters to let me do just evangelistic work?"

She clapped her hands, happier than I had seen her in a long time. "I think that would be wonderful!"

"Remember," I said, "We've been living off a salary. There won't be one, if I do this. No salary, no car, no certainty of anything — "

She didn't care. "I'd rather live with a poor preacher than ever have to live with a wealthy man that's become a politician."

"Now what are you talking about, a politician?"

She says, "I didn't tell you, but there were two fellows here. They wanted to elect you on the School Board. And the very next week, they came again, and wanted to elect you on the City Council. The next thing would be the Provincial Council, and then you'd go to Parliament. And then what would I have? A man who cannot be faithful to the call of God on his life." She wiped her hands on her apron. "I'd ten times rather suffer with you in the ministry than have to suffer the treatment of a wicked man."

I gave her a hug, and before long we moved to Johannesburg, and rented a home there in very poor circumstances, with Anna taking in boarders to help meet the rent. But the Lord was ever faithful, and always undertook. And gradually I became a leader in the Pentecostal movement.

Years later, I met some of the men who had been on the board of directors. "Mr. du Plessis," they asked me, "aren't you sorry now that you left?"

"Oh, no," I laughed, "look where the Lord is about to have me go now! To America!" I paused. "I couldn't have gone anywhere if I'd stayed in the print shop. No, I think I took the way of the Lord, and I have no regrets at all."

"Well, one thing is certain," they replied. "You took over a bankrupt company, and you did not leave it bankrupt. You saved a lot of people their jobs, and the print shop is still going places."

"Well, I'm glad. And you know, it was a valuable time for me, too. For I learned that, while we may not always be well off financially, we will be spiritually, if we follow the Lord's plan, whatever the cost."

How does living by faith equate with the so-called 'Blessing Ministry'?

There is a popular move today, to take the promise contained in Mark 11:23-24, "Whatever you ask for in prayer, believe that you receive it, and you will," and to build a spiritual way of life around it. They now give God orders, claiming and believing for everything under the sun.

But a long time ago, Sam Shoemaker told me: "Never preach on a text, if you haven't experienced it." I tried verse 24, and nothing happened; my checks bounced. And I said, "Lord, I get no results from this text, why? It's a promise, isn't it?"

Yes.

"Then Lord, will you increase my faith?"

There is nothing wrong with your faith. Verse 25 is your problem.

I looked it up: "And when you stand praying (and asking), forgive, if you have ought against any, so that your Father, who also is in heaven, may forgive you your trespasses." I saw that the former verse was conditional upon the latter. "Dear Lord, help me; I've got so many 'oughts' against so many 'anys'." And that was when I first discovered the mountain of unforgiveness that needed to be cast into the sea of forgetfulness. And *that* brought me to repentance and humility — without which, praying and believing is little more than presumption.

Too many would-be faith-shepherds are starting churches on presumption. Not long ago, two of them came to the West Coast from the heartland of the "blessing ministry," and went straight to the Cadillac dealer. They told him that they had been called by God to minister to the vacationers at Lake Tahoe, and they would each need a Cadillac, because that was a Cadillac world. The dealer said, "Well, that's fine; who's going to pay for them? Have you got the money?"

"No, the Lord will take care of that."

"Well, that's fine," replied the dealer, "but I'll need a down-payment. Have you got that?"

"No, the Lord will take care of that."

Something about them must have struck the dealer, because he said, "I'll tell you what: I'm going to try you two out. I will give you each a car, but you will have one month to come up with the down-payment."

When a month went by, and they could not make the down-payment, he took back the cars, and these two would-be blessing-ministers had to walk away from that dealership on foot. I can only wonder what sort of taste they left in people's mouths.

9

70 x 7

If the author had but one message to bring, it would be on the importance of forgiveness. Early in life, he learned how it could change everything, and he has been a living example of its power ever since.

Where did forgiveness begin for you?

In the beginning, I was not a forgiving person. I knew firsthand about the fights between the Pentecostals and the Protestants, because I was in the thick of them. For instance, when I went to a Dutch Reformed Church and heard the minister attack our movement and call it false and an evil thing, because it was causing disturbances in the Protestant churches, I sat there and thought: why is he a Christian? Jesus caused disturbance in the synagogue and the Temple.

I *was* concerned about the prayer that Jesus taught His disciples: forgive us as we forgive others, but I assumed it applied only to the body of believers that I happened to be in. We were born again, and others were not, and so I considered them a mission field and not a Christian body.

I had lost sight of the truth, that churches were still churches, and they still had Christ. I had taken the Pentecostal attitude of "come ye out from among them," because *they* had been pushing *us* out. They had been expelling us, and to us it was more respectable to come out than to be pushed out.

As I grew older, I stopped fighting, but I still had not forgiven the churches. And then I came to realize that my "word of wisdom," my "word of knowledge," and all my preaching were not helping anyone. Because I was not preaching in love to the people. I had not learned to forgive and love. If you forgive, then you have to substitute love for the old feeling.

Then one day, the Lord said to me: *What Smith Wigglesworth told you is soon to come about.*

"But, Lord, he told me to go to the old-line denominations, and they're dead."

I never arrange for funerals. You had better raise the dead.

"Lord, they're enemies."

Then love them.

"How can I love people that I don't agree with?"

Forgive them.

"I can't justify them."

I never gave any child of mine authority to justify anybody. I gave you full authority to forgive them. That's all you have.

So I forgave the Protestants for all they had done to the poor Pentecostals, and I forgave the Catholics for all they had done to the poor Protestants. Then the Pentecostals wanted to know who had given me the authority to do that, and so I had to forgive the Pentecostals!

I live by forgiveness. And I love by forgiveness, because they can do anything they want to; I just forgive them.

Is forgiveness only for Christians, or can it work in the world?

I once asked a judge who was a Christian and had been on the bench for forty years: "Were you usually able to settle a case, when you had the necessary witnesses and evidence?"

He thought for a moment, before answering. "You know, when I look back, I realize I almost never really settled a case. I only helped them to come to an agreement to stop litigation, and to stop spending money."

"But you know," I replied, "that God Himself abandoned the law and on Calvary introduced forgiveness. That is God's new way. The law — no law — could save anybody, or help anybody. But forgiveness is always successful."

He shook his head sadly. "I dare not speak of forgiveness in court. I'm a judge, and on the bench I've got to judge." And then he smiled. "But I can invite the disputing parties into my chambers, and there is where I can really settle cases by forgiveness."

I nodded. "Thank you! You have helped me to see it in relation to our own situation. What a pity that the Church, instead of preaching forgiveness, became judges, or prosecutors." I sighed. "In fact, that was my own job for years. I thought it was my duty to prosecute everybody, to get them straightened out, according to the law. Why, I made even the Sermon on the Mount a law: 'You've got to live according to the Sermon on the Mount

— that's what Jesus taught!' But I had forgotten that Jesus did not teach that in order to make it a law; He taught that it was the consequence of a new birth." And I thanked the judge again, for further clarifying my perspective.

Must we forgive everyone? For everything?

Yes, even the Nazis, for the Holocaust. I said this once, a long time ago, and Loren Cunningham heard me. He was just a young boy then, twelve years old, but he took it and decided that he would follow my example. (He never dreamed that he would have to follow me through expulsion and all the rest.) Accompanied by teams of young people from his Youth With a Mission, Loren had made a specialty of evangelizing at Olympics, and in 1972, he acquired a beautiful castle in Germany, for his headquarters at the Munich Olympics. He had some of his best YWAM people with him, strong teams with a lot of field experience and good preparation — but they were making no headway; they could not win a single convert.

In despair, they called a prayer meeting and wept before the Lord. And Loren, sensing that the Lord held him personally responsible, cried out, "Lord, speak to me: what is wrong? We had success in Mexico, at the Olympics there; we've had success everywhere. You have blessed us; you have provided the facilities and all the equipment we need. And yet here we cannot move. Why?"

And then he heard the Lord: *You have not forgiven Hitler.*

"But Lord, Hitler is dead."

*Not in your mind. You still hold all Germans respon-
sible for the Holocaust. All Germans did not agree with
Hitler, but you do not know that. Unless you forgive
them, you will never help them to recover.*

Loren told the others what the Lord had revealed to
him, and together they forgave Hitler, and everyone else
involved. Immediately things changed. God blessed their
ministry mightily, opening doors which had previously
been closed to them, and enabling them to win many
converts.

Loren told me that the lesson changed the Youth With
a Mission approach, from then on. "You can be sure that
now, before any mission, we ask God to search our hearts
for anything, known or unknown, we might be holding
against those we seek to help."

Must forgiveness, then, be always unconditional?

"Walk in love," the Apostle writes — I am not crippled;
I must *walk*. And the walk must be in love. This is where
the Lord helped me, when He said: *You cannot love
people, if you have not first completely, unconditionally,
forgiven them. You have too many conditions.*

That unconditional forgiveness did not come in the
beginning. (Thank God, He didn't tell me everything at
once; I would have given up!) It was revealed step by
step, and the latest was when He said: *On Calvary, Jesus
made no conditions. He simply said, "Father, forgive
them, for they know not what they do." Your forgiveness
is still: "if they do this, if they do that." You still expect*

*some sign of repentance, and then you'll forgive. You
must forgive people, no matter how they behave, no
matter whether you think they are worthy. You just
forgive. And if you forgive them, you can love them. And
if you love them, you can beat any enemy. But you will
never win your enemies, if you don't love them.*

How do we make enemies? By finding fault with each
other. By hurting each other in speech and in our
thoughts. So, I had to learn to "walk in love, as Christ
loved us and gave Himself for us, a sacrifice unto God."
That's why I like the verse: "Hereby perceive we the love
of God, because He has laid down His life for us, and we
ought to lay down our lives for the brethren" (I John
3:16). That kind of love is unconditional.

When I began to see this, things began to happen that
I'd never seen before. I had no way of knowing what the
effect would be, but I could see that Jesus on the Cross
had granted unconditional forgiveness to the Jews who
shouted, "Crucify Him!" and to the Romans, Jew and
gentile — that means all humanity. He had forgiven once
and for all, and that was sealed with His blood.

He was doing this, even as His blood poured out, and
that is why we now say He cleanses us. True, but the
cleansing comes when we accept His unconditional
forgiveness. Our own forgiveness must be unconditional,
too; we must not forgive people just because they do
something that pleases us. We must forgive our enemies.

An example: Here comes a man called Saul of Tarsus,
wreaking havoc with the Church, which he found not in
the temple, but from house to house. Stephen, who had
been chosen as a deacon, had become a powerful
evangelist, and Saul said that if this young fellow carries
on like this, he'll convert all Israel. We must put him out
of the way. So he gathered a mob and stoned him, and

when Stephen saw the end was coming, he fell to his knees. He saw heaven open, and he saw Christ standing. Christ stood up to welcome him home, but before he went, he said: "Father, lay not this sin to their charge." That was unconditional forgiveness.

And what happened? Jesus had taught that what you bind on earth shall be bound in heaven, and what you liberate on earth shall be liberated in heaven. Here, Stephen liberated Saul of Tarsus, the leader of the mob, from judgment. "Lay not this sin to their charge" — that caused the King of Kings, the Lord of Lords, the Prince of Glory, the Mighty Saviour, to come from His throne all the way down to the road to Damascus, to arrest Saul of Tarsus. He made him His prisoner, and Paul always spoke of himself as a prisoner of Christ.

This example of the most dangerous enemy of the Church, who became its champion, gave me the grace and courage to forgive. I don't care how much they fight the Charismatic Movement or what they do to the Pentecostals, I forgive them. And I have seen some of the greatest fighters of the opposition, even those who said we are of the devil, become champions of the movement. The Lord can change people! In fact, He said to me: *You can turn all your enemies into champions, if you will forgive them so unconditionally that they cannot escape it.*

Does that explain your lapel pin — "70 x 7"?

Yes, and it helps remind me that forgiveness is a continuing affair. Because the temptation to stop forgiving is always present. Incidentally, I have had enough of these pins made, including a slightly smaller size for women, to give to anyone who asks for them. Anyone wishing one, and they are not available anywhere else, should write to me at:

P. O. Box 2500
Pasadena, California 91102

10

TRUST AND OBEY

The more one walks in the Spirit, the more he or she realizes that his entire life boils down to that simple (and oh, so difficult) commandment: trust and obey. We practice it and practice it, and as we gradually get better at it, He gradually entrusts us with more and more responsibility — but only so long as we demonstrate that we are worthy of that trust. The author has spent more than half a century putting his trust and obedience into practice. He has been given unique and often crucial responsibility, yet he would be the first to admit that he is still learning.

What is the secret of being led by the Spirit?

I wait. The Lord must tell me the time, and the persons I am to see — first this, and then the other, and so on. Some people think that kind of guidance is rather crazy, but it works for me, because every time I am obedient to it, I have results. I could tell you of the most amazing experiences — like the time I was involved with the National Council of Churches and had come to New

York, to their headquarters on Riverside Drive.

By the way, when the Lord tells me to go, I don't make appointments, so when I had seen the persons I wanted to see, here was lunch time coming, and I had no plans. Well, I thought, I could go to their cafeteria, but then I would meet so many that I knew, I would never get away. So I just stood there and said, "Lord, I've got no guidance beyond this; what must I do?"

Cross the street and go to Union Seminary.

"Oh, I know where that is," I murmured, "just around the corner," and I walked there, strangely without a concern of what I was going to do, once I got there. I walked in, and behind the desk was a black man who said, "Good day, sir, what can I do for you?"

Suddenly, I realized: what could I tell him? "Um, I don't know," I stammered, aware of the impression I must be making. "I've come to see somebody." At that instant, the name of a professor whom I had met before came in my mind, and with more confidence, I said that I would like to speak to Professor so-and-so.

"All right," he said, "I'll get him on the phone," and when he did, he handed me the receiver.

"Hello?" I could hear the professor asking.

"This is David du Plessis," I managed.

"Where are you?"

"Down in the office."

"What office?"

"Your front office; I'm right here."

"You just arrived?"

"Yes."

"Oh, thank God! You are a godsend! I'll be right down!" And without explaining further, he hung up. A few moments later, he appeared breathless and beaming.

"We have a faculty luncheon today, and our speaker's copped out; he's sick or something. Anyway, we desperately need a speaker, and now we have one: you."

So he took me in, and I had the privilege of addressing that whole faculty. I had a great time, and truly the Lord helped me that day. At the end, as I said goodbye, they gave me a standing ovation. I never dreamed there would be anything further to come of that supernatural episode, but God is the Master Economist: nothing is ever wasted, and no one can ever foresee the full effect of our acts of obedience.

A couple of years later, I received an invitation to a Methodist seminary in Wheaton, Illinois, which had recently joined with another. But I did not know exactly what they were, or why they had invited me. When I got there, it was late, and when I questioned the faculty member who met me at the airport, all he could tell me was that I would be staying in the apartment, where important visitors stayed.

The next morning, I attended their chapel service and was impressed by the homily I heard there, thinking that I really must meet that man. After the service, I found that I had been given the assignment of speaking to a class on alienation, and when I met the class, there was a professor from the South there, who was to speak on reconciliation. He would speak this day, and I would speak the next, but in the meantime, when he finished, the students and I were to question him and critique his speech.

I said, "I have enjoyed this speech. I know a bit about reconciliation: I was born an alien — to my parents. They didn't understand their first-born, and I surely did not understand them! But as I grew up and got saved, I realized that I had to become reconciled with my parents. And now I've learned to be reconciled to all people — by forgiveness and by love."

The next day, it was my turn. I gave my testimony, and afterwards the professor said, "I have never heard a Pentecostal. If what this man has taught us this morning is what Pentecostals really believe, then I've been badly misinformed. Because I have heard that they are people who always quarrel with others, and always think that everybody else is wrong. Which is hardly conducive to reconciliation."

That noon, I was invited to lunch with the president and the dean. As we finished, the president said, "You cannot imagine how happy we are to have you here! We sense that this seminary is on the brink of something exciting. When we came here two years ago, the place was so liberal that one of the professors interfered with the girls, and we were able to dismiss him." He smiled at me. "The man whose homily you admired in chapel this morning, is his replacement, and we think that in him we've hit the jackpot! By the way, you'll be having dinner at his home tonight, instead of in the cafeteria."

But now I was baffled and finally had to ask: "You two speak as if you know me."

"Yes, that's why we invited you. When we had difficulty with that professor, we had to decide: are we going liberal, or are we going spiritual? And we decided: we'll go spiritual. Now who will we get to bring us into the fundamentals on a sound basis? David du Plessis, of course."

I couldn't help asking why.

"Do you remember one day, a couple of years ago, when you spoke at a faculty luncheon at Union Seminary?" I nodded. "Well, that day, after you finished speaking, both of us realized that we were changed men.

We don't know what all happened, but we were certainly born again, and for the first time understood the new birth. The Lord met us there. And you had made clear what we needed to do next. He that is Jesus, the Saviour, the Lamb of God that takes away sin, is also the Baptizer. So we two prayed together, and He baptized us in the Holy Spirit."

I was nonplussed; without any further teaching, that message had changed the lives of these two men.

"Well, now," the president went on, "how were we going to get this place spiritual? The students were nice boys, and there were some young couples here that were baptized in the Holy Spirit. But they had no leader. How could we turn it spiritual? And then we looked at each other and said, 'What about David du Plessis?' And so, here you are."

"All right," I said, "now I know. But does this mean I have an absolutely free hand?"

"Yes. As far as we're concerned you can turn the entire institution Pentecostal, if you can manage it. But in order not to make it too conspicuous, we got this other professor to speak for the South, knowing that you came from South Africa, and would understand him and the feelings of the blacks and so on."

"Fine, then where I would like to begin is with the informal, one-hour prayer groups that some of the students apparently have in the evenings, before they close up."

Permission was granted, and the Holy Spirit went to work. The course of the seminary altered significantly then, and when I finally left, I could not help reflecting on all that had followed that single instance of blind obedience, when I had stood on that corner in New York, and had asked God where to go next.

How did you ever learn to 'Trust and Obey' so totally?

I had been learning it all my life. But I guess the most extraordinary, sustained lesson — the one which would set the pattern for the rest of my life — came after the World Conference in Zurich, Switzerland, in 1947. It had been our first World Conference since before the war, and it was a great success. I made many lasting friendships and received a number of standing invitations to speak, both in Europe and America. As it happened, I was on sabbatical (I had taken no time off in years), and so was able to accept some of these invitations.

I went to Sweden first, where it was the beginning of summer, and time for their great annual outdoor tent meetings. Thousands upon thousands would come and stay in tents, and it was a glorious time. From there, I went to another conference in a port city in Norway, and was due to go to Finland next, but when I was ready to leave, I could not find Dr. Souemela, who was to be my host in Helsinki, where he and his wife were both doctors. Worse, he had not given me his address, so I had no way of getting in touch with him, once I got over there.

I was due to fly to Oslo, for another tent meeting, after which I was to fly to Helsinki, so there was nothing to do but go to the airport . . . maybe I would be able to get his address from one of the other Pentecostal brethren returning to Finland. When I checked in at the counter, they said, "Oh, you're the man we couldn't find; you had already checked out of the hotel. Your flight has been cancelled." The agent looked at me. "But don't worry; we have another plane going two hours later. We can put you on that one." I wasn't worried (happy is the man

who can endure what he cannot cure), and now he gave
me a choice: "You can wait here, or we can give you a
taxi ride back into town. All you'll have to do is be sure to
catch the hotel limousine back out here for the next
flight."

I chose to go back, and the taxi dropped me at the city
terminal. There I stood, and all of a sudden I wondered
what on earth had made me want to come back into
town? I could not speak the language and knew no one in
this city . . . . How foolish, I thought; now I will just have
to wait here, instead of at the airport.

I walked out into the street and looked around. Spying
an inviting little park with beautiful flower beds, I made
my way over there. And as I stood marveling at these
little sunbursts of nature's coloring, I forgot my miseries.
I began to walk along on the paths in the park, now
thoroughly enjoying the flowers and having a little
holiday, as it were. Arriving at a street, I hesitated, not
knowing which way to go next, when somebody touched
my arm. Turning around, I was surprised to find no one
there; indeed, there was not another person in sight.

"What?" I murmured aloud, "Lord, did *You* alert
me?"

Yes. Cross over, in the direction you are now facing.

So I crossed over and stood there, waiting for some
indication of where I should go next. Nothing came, and
I began to wonder why I had crossed the street. Abruptly,
there was another touch on my arm. *Cross again.*

Go back across the same street which I had just finished
crossing? What was the point of that? Was I going to go
back and forth across this street for an hour, like some
poor old man who had lost his mind? Such are the
thoughts with which Satan harasses us, when we seek to
be blindly obedient.

I turned around and went back across the street again, walking slowly and staring at the pavement, and concentrating inwardly for the slightest further guidance — but there was none. When I reached the curb, I looked up — and noticed a familiar figure approaching, briefcase in hand and eyes on the sidewalk in front of him. "Dr. Souemela?" I called out.

He looked up and exclaimed, "Oh, glory to God, at last I've found you! Do you know, the Lord would not let me ride with my baggage to the boat? He said to send it ahead and to walk down to the wharf. It made no sense at all — until now."

I smiled. "You know what He had to do with me? He had to cancel my plane. There was no plane when I got to the airport to go to Oslo, and that's why I'm here." I walked with him to the boat, and then caught the limousine back to the airport. I was much in awe of how God would orchestrate "coincidence," if we would trust Him enough to obey the gentlest nudge. But I never dreamed that this was only the opening curtain!

Miracles of coincidence accompanied me everywhere I went on that sabbatical, each one enlarging my trust a little bit more. It was enlarged substantially, when I reached London. I thought that now I would soon be going home, but God had other plans. He said: *Prepare and arrange for a seat to go to America.*

And so, for a whole day, I walked from one travel agent to the next, trying to get a berth on a boat. But at that time, it seemed that every American left in England was trying to get back home, and there was not one space available. In despair, and a bit angry, I stopped and stood at the edge of the great intersection of Piccadilly Circus, and prayed, "Dear Lord, you must have known there is no hope of getting on any ship."

As sure as the Lord was there, I heard Him say, *I did not say book a berth; I said book a seat!*

"But Lord, that means an airplane! I haven't got the money!" And then I reminded myself how far you can go wrong, by not following the Lord's guidance implicitly. All right, I would book a seat — but the day was almost over; lights were already coming on.

Suddenly, across the Circus, I saw the name of the company that had arranged my seat on the plane from South Africa. I walked over there, and it was still open. Walking in, I said to the man behind the counter, "I know your company operates everywhere; do you, by any chance, know of one of their customers, a fellow named David du Plessis?"

"Why, yes, we have his file here, somewhere; he's a VIP."

Trying to look casual, I said, "You handle all types of travel and represent all kinds of firms?" He nodded. "Well," I went on, flipping through a brochure, "would there be any chance of David du Plessis getting a seat on a plane to America?"

"No," the agent replied, "not for a couple of months. Everybody wants to get out of England just now."

"But there are such things as cancellations," I persisted. "Couldn't there be one?"

"Yes, one could come, but I usually build up a waiting list, and it would go to the first person on that list."

"Thank you," I replied, smiling, "I just thought I'd check. I'm David du Plessis."

He looked up, startled. "Why didn't you tell me? I should never have divulged that information."

"Don't worry, you're not in trouble. I've got to go to Manchester for the weekend. I'm going to pray that the

Lord will record me as a stand-by or something, to get a seat on a plane." As I spoke, he took out my file, and noted where I would be staying in Manchester and Blackheath.

Off I went to Manchester, where I had some great meetings with Nelson Parr, who had a large Assembly Church. They gave me a most generous offering of 50 pounds and my train fare to Blackheath. When I got there, I was met by Pastor Barnes, and the moment we stepped in his home, his wife asked, "You look a little weary; would you like a cup of tea?"

"Oh, yes," I nodded, "in England, tea is always welcome."

A few moments later, she returned with a steaming cup and said, "By the way, there was a call for you just now — from the City, something about a seat on a plane."

"That must be the travel agent," I murmured.

"Shall I call him back?" she asked.

"No, no. First, let me have my tea."

Before I could finish, the phone rang again. It was the agent, and when I got on, he said, "You must have prayed hard! I've got a seat for you."

"When must I pick up the ticket?"

"In one hour, I'm afraid; that's why I called back so soon."

"Oh, no," I said, "I'm out in Blackheath. I'll never make it; can you give me more time?"

He hesitated for a moment, then said, "All right, we'll make it an hour and a half. But we can't give you a minute more."

"Thank you, that will have to be enough," and I rang off. Turning around, I said, "Sister Barnes, I'm in trouble.

I've asked this man to reserve a seat to America. He's got one, but I haven't got any money. I don't suppose you have any?"

"I'm sorry," she said, "we exist on ration cards; we've got nothing."

"Um, any chance of getting some from the church?"

"Not without a board meeting, I'm afraid."

"Well, I guess there's nothing to do but to go to London and talk to the agent."

"Without money?"

"Yes, what else can I do? The Lord knows my situation; He may already have some money coming from somewhere."

Mrs. Barnes looked at me, almost as if she were sorry for me, for entertaining such a vain hope. Then she remembered something. "Wait a minute: the postman has just been here." She went out and came back in a moment later with several small brown envelopes, of the sort they put bills in. "Now here's one for you,' she said, surprised, handing one to me. "Perhaps the money you need is in there."

"Sister Barnes," I replied, "this is no time for jokes. I'm sweating." I opened it, and here was a check from a church that I had recently visited, and the man who sent it wrote: "At eleven o'clock at night, the Lord woke me up and said, *Get up, make out a check for this amount to David du Plessis, and mail it before midnight, so that it will reach him in the morning.* If you need the enclosed, then God spoke to me. If you don't need it, just send it back and forget about it."

I literally ran for the train, got the first one in to London, went straight to the agency office, and out of breath asked the agent, if he still had the ticket. He did.

"Good!" I gasped, "here's my check," and I handed him the brown envelope, as he pulled out the ticket. Looking at it, I could not believe my eyes: the amount written on it was the exact amount of the check!

"Um — this check is made out from a church," the agent said, in a way that indicated that he was not happy about it.

"Oh, it's all right," I said, "it's a big old church, very well-to-do. But I'll vouch for it," I added, trying to look like someone who had a personal account and was used to vouching for things.

The agent seemed to make up his mind. "Very well, sir, you'll be flying with Sabena, out of Brussels tomorrow."

Once again, knowing that I had a sum total of 50 pounds sterling, the Lord undertook to get me to Brussels on time, and a day later, I was in New York. There, of course, was an office of the Assemblies of God, and my old friend Bob McGlassen. I told Bob I was hoping to get to Grand Rapids, where the Assemblies were going to have their General Council meeting, and I shared with him that I sensed that the Lord might be preparing me to move to America. For at the World Conference, I had experienced the camaraderie and close fellowship that the U. S. leaders had for one another, and to my surprise discovered that they had nothing like it back home, nothing that brought them together. Well, perhaps the Lord would have me give talks in this country, and would use me as a catalyst to create inter-church or inter-state fellowship, where none existed.

As we were talking, into the Assemblies office walked Fannie B. Smith, an old missionary in South Africa who had been in the States on furlough, and was on her way back. She stared at me and then exclaimed, "Well, I never! I thought you were in South Africa, or on your way back, like me."

"No, the Lord told me to come here."

"Well," she said, "I know how you travel, David, and the Lord has just told me to give you some money." With that, she took some bills out of her purse — just enough to get me to Grand Rapids.

Listening to the *clickety-clack* of the train wheels that evening, I thanked God for the ongoing lesson He was teaching me; I had never experienced or heard of anything like it, and so, smiling and sensing His closeness, I shut my eyes and drifted off to sleep. I cannot remember whether I dreamed, but if I did, it could only have paled in comparison to the dream I was living. And it went on.

When we got to Grand Rapids, I checked into the headquarters hotel. The brethren were all happy to see me, and asked me to speak at one of the meetings. Afterwards, they gave me an honorarium which was just enough to cover my hotel bill. Then a brother invited me to come to Detroit and speak in his church there, but once again I was penniless. Detroit was not that far, but it might as well have been on another continent. No matter, if God wanted me there . . . .

Standing in the check-out line, I recognized the man behind me. It turned out that we had both been at the World Conference, and I told him, "I've been asked to speak in Detroit, and I don't have the money to fly there; you wouldn't happen to know of anyone driving there?"

"Boy," he said, "there's a couple from Detroit here who talked to me about you, and they were so anxious to have you, I think they would be delighted to take you there." He introduced me, and I got a free ride to

Detroit, right to the parsonage of the pastor who had invited me.

He was delighted to see me, and knowing of my desire to make my way to the west coast, speaking as I went, he told me that he had arranged a huge meeting for me. "We're going to take a love offering, David, and there should be hundreds of dollars — enough to see you all the way out there, and then some." But one hour before the meeting, the heavens opened up, and we experienced the most violent rainstorm you could ever imagine. A total of 70 hardy souls braved the elements to hear what the Lord would give me to say, and my host was thunderstruck (so to speak). "Brother David, this is a calamity!"

"No, no," I reassured him, "it is the Lord. These are the people He brought here, and He will look after me perfectly, as He has been right along." And He did; their love offering was just enough to take me to Chicago, which was where I had planned to go next, anyway.

I spoke in a church I knew in Chicago, where they took a love offering for me that saw me to Minneapolis, with 25¢ left over. But in those days it took only a dime to make a phone call, and so I called a man I knew there. He was home and free, and glad to hear from me. He said he would come and get me, and so I spent a nickel on a cup of coffee, and waited. Ten minutes became twenty and then forty, and I began to realize that something must have happened to him, and of course he had no way of calling me in the coffee shop . . . I had one dime left, and no one else to call.

But I had something else left, something that God wanted me to be completely rid of: pride. Because, also in the station coffee shop was a man I had befriended in Chicago, an Englishman named Fred Squire. He kept asking me when I was leaving, and finally I spent my last dime's worth of pride and told him the truth: I was on my way to Seattle, where I had been invited to hold meetings, but I had run completely out of money.

Instead of scorning me, he was delighted! "Good! Now I have a chance to do something for you!" With that, he called his pastor, whose reaction was the same, and they gave me a check which covered my fare to Seattle.

In each place that I spoke along the way, if they had been at the World Conference — and most of them had, which was how I happened to know so many Yanks — they would ask me to "preach that sermon again on wheat and chaff," which had been my keynote message for the Conference. But in Seattle, the pastor asked me *not* to preach on it, because he had come home and used it himself.

My stay in Seattle provided me with enough funds to get down to the Angelus Temple at Echo Park in Los Angeles, the famed headquarters church of the Foursquare Gospel denomination. Howard Rusthoi was pastor in those days, and he invited me to come and do a week of meetings. When I arrived, he explained that their board of directors had already arranged a number of other things, so he could give me only one evening in the Temple. "But if you don't mind, I've arranged for you to speak the rest of the week in different churches — some are ours, some are Assemblies, and so on. You're booked every night, if that's all right."

"That's fine," I said, "and it's probably the Lord. Because this way I will reach folks I might not have, otherwise."

One night, during my stay in Los Angeles, the Lord woke me up at 4:00 and said: *Look at your calendar.* I did — and realized that in thirty days I had to be back in South Africa. "Thank You, Lord, for reminding me." I

had gotten so caught up in what I was doing, I had totally
forgotten about time. And now He said: *Cable South
Africa and resign, and follow me.* That was it. I was
stunned, but there was no questioning what He had said
— and no chance of persuading Him to change His mind.

I was grateful that my wise old friend, Donald Gee,
was preaching at the Temple at the time, and I went to
see him, and to discuss it with him. "Well," he said, "you
may be surprised, but I'm not. For some time, I've had
the feeling that the Lord wants you for a world ministry.
What Wigglesworth told you could mean nothing less,
and a world ministry means leaving South Africa."

All right, so now what to do . . . . Trust and obey: I
sent the cable of resignation. And now Satan began to
harass me: What would I be doing? How was I going to
support my family? We've got a home there; what about
that? Well, we could rent it, and that would cover the
mortgage payments . . . . I planned and planned. But
always in the back of my mind loomed the largest question of all: how was I going to tell Anna?

The Lord had that answer, too. The next morning, He
told me: *Now, cable Anna to sell everything, and prepare
to come to Switzerland.*

What! For years, Anna had made no secret of her
loathing of change and uprooting. "You can travel, and
go all over the world, if you like," she would say, "but I
am staying in South Africa." And now, I was to cable
her . . . .

Trust and obey. I sent the cable. Almost immediately
afterwards, I received a letter from her, posted before she
could have gotten the cable. In it she wrote: "When I
learned from the head office of your resignation, I was
upset. But the Lord has spoken to me and said, *If I want*

to use David, how can you stand in his way? So, I have decided: where you go, I go; where you sleep, I sleep. I will go wherever He may lead you, but on one condition: we burn the bridges and sell everything, so that we have nothing to come back to in South Africa. There must be no lingering attachments."

Poor Anna! She had to sell the car, sell the house, put the furniture up for auction, and dozens of other heart-wrenching things, for South Africa was all we had ever known. It was all that our parents or grand-parents had ever known; in fact, our roots went so deep, that on my side, the Du Plessis name went all the way back to the seventeenth century, when the cousin of Armand Jean du Plessis, duc de Richelieu, left Paris (shortly after his ambitious cousin became the legendary Cardinal Richelieu), to begin a plantation in South Africa.

It would have been hard enough for Anna alone, but by this time we had four children, none of them old enough fully to appreciate why the Du Plessis family suddenly had to leave all their friends and family behind. But, by God's grace, she did it, and in the meantime, I was over in Switzerland, trusting and obeying, as the Lord arranged a place for us to live.

11

GOD AND THE PENTECOSTALS

For many years, the author led the Pentecostal Movement in South Africa, as its General Secretary, before joining the staff of the World Conference and emigrating to America. He learned many valuable lessons of leadership in those early days, which are relevant today.

What is your greatest difficulty in Pentecostal churches today?

Jesus once said to the Pharisees: "Your traditions have made the Word of God of none effect" (Matthew 15:6), and I find that today tradition is my great difficulty. While I was speaking in Bolivia, a Catholic bishop came to the meeting, and after I'd spoken for awhile, he said to me, "Now, tell me: what do you find your greatest difficulty in your travels?"

"Traditions, always traditions." And that is true of all denominations; in fact, I cannot find a local church that has no traditions. And the Pentecostals are not exempt;

once proud of leaving traditions behind, over the years they have developed their own.

The last church in the world that I would ever want to be the pastor of, would be one where I had to follow the founder-pastor. For he has laid down his traditions, and I could never do well, unless I did things the way he did them. And this I see, too, in the Pentecostal Chruch. One of the oldest pioneers in South Africa said to me, "When I retire or pass away, I'd like you to be the pastor of my church."

"Why?" I asked him.

"Well, I know you, I love you, and I like your teaching."

"Well, then, let me tell you: I will not accept, because I don't know what you would do."

He smiled. "I'd just stay and help you."

"That's exactly what I don't want."

"What would you want?"

"I'd want you to move 500 miles away, so that people couldn't see you, and I wouldn't have to worry about you."

He chuckled and said, "I never thought of that."

I nodded. "Yes, that is the difficulty."

"What can I do, then? I feel I must retire — can you find a pastor that will, you think, do the job?"

I smiled. "I've already got one in mind." As Secretary, I knew of a pastor who was just five years younger than him. They had both been pioneers in the movement, and I thought that if I put that man there, they would get along fine, and he would help them get over the hump. So I did, and sure enough, it worked out perfectly, because they were both almost the same age, and had been together for so many years in the field.

How do you compare the Pentecostal
and the Charismatic Movement?

When I am asked that, I recall what occurred at the
wedding at Cana: when the master of ceremonies tasted
the water which Jesus had turned into wine. He marveled
and said to the bridegroom; "anyone sets before his guests
the best wine first, and then that which is worse. But you
have kept the best wine till the last!" (John 2:10). To me,
that means that Pentecost and the early days were good,
but what we have today is the best wine. It's better, and
it is far more abundant than what they had in the beginning. As Jesus predicted, I can write a Book of Acts of the
Holy Spirit in my lifetime that would eclipse the Acts of
the Apostles.

Looking at Christian history, what there was in
Jerusalem and from then on was always just a small
thing, even the Reformation — it took ages, and it did
not advance the cause of unity; it increased the divisions.
It still does. Even Pentecost did not bring about the unity
that one would think would easily come. We had been so
used to dividing in the Protestant world, that we kept on
doing the same thing. But the Pentecostals' trouble was
not that they kept dividing; they were not in unity in the
beginning, because the Holy Spirit did not do everything
from one center. It happened everywhere. And so you
cannot say that we are divided; we're merely separated
by the backgrounds that we come out of. What was
more, we had to deal with the Church around us — the
old churches that we belonged to.

Then, from 1950 on, there is evidently in the world a
new atmosphere — spiritually, all of a sudden there is a
move. Up to that time, missionaries had struggled to win

a few converts; now, they flock in hundreds of thousands to meetings. And this to me is proof that the Spirit is indeed moving upon all flesh.

I once asked Brother Wigglesworth if he had Scripture, regarding the Pentecostal Movement, and he referred me to Acts 6:7, "And the Word of God increased and the number of disciples multiplied in Jerusalem greatly." "That was the first wave," he said. "But here, listen to this: 'And a great company of priests were obedient to the faith.' That was the second wave." In the first decades of this century, a great company had come to believe — except the ministry, the ministers from the churches. Our old revival was with the poor, but now the spirituality has come from educated, learned theologians. And look at all the ministers now coming in! In the Catholic church, it really began in the seminaries, with the ministry and with the educated.

Are we now experiencing the last wave?

I believe so. In my fourscore years, I've seen several moves of the Spirit. I do not believe that there is a great revival or a new wave still to come. This *is* Joel's last wave. And this is where Joel's prophecy is fulfilled, for we live in a culture now, where there is equality of the sexes. It was not the Holy Spirit who brought it about; it was the circumstances of the world. But God knew that this would be the culture of this day. And so Joel said, "Your sons *and* daughters shall prophesy. . . servants *and* handmaidens." In Joel's own day, that would have been absolute heresy, because Levitical law recognized only men, not women and children. So, we've got a new culture and a new manifestation of the Spirit. I am quite satisfied that this is the last wave.

Why were you expelled from the Pentecostal Movement?

When the Lord tells me to do something, I do it. And sometimes, I cannot get anyone to agree. My own Pentecostal brethren disfellowshipped me because they couldn't agree with me. The Lord had told me to reach out to all denominations, and I had to obey. The Pentecostal leadership demanded that I cease and desist. I had to tell them, I'm sorry, I cannot comply with your demands. If I listen to you, I've got to stop what I'm doing, or I've got to resign. And I'll never resign from any church. For if I do, they'll want to know what's wrong with me or what's wrong with the church. And there's nothing wrong with me or my church. It is just that I have received marching orders from the Lord that are not approved of by their council, because of their traditions.

That was how, in 1962, the Assemblies of God expelled me, in a sense. They gave me notice: "Your ministry in the Assemblies of God is hereby terminated." They had gotten me out of the World Conference as Secretary, and now they had gotten me out of their ministry.

And now I understood what the Lord had been referring to, when He had said: *Are you prepared to lose your whole status? Are you prepared to lose your ministry?*

I had argued with Him then. "But, Lord, that's all I live for!"

Yes, and you must not worship your ministry. You must not be in idolatry. Worship me.

"All right, Lord, I'm prepared to lose my ministry. But what will I live for?"

I can take care of that.

Yet it was hard to remember that, at first, when they put me out of the Assemblies; all I could think was, "I'm *nothing!*"

Yes, said the Lord, when my thoughts had calmed down enough to hear Him, *you must first be nothing, before you can be all things to all men. As long as you are somebody, you will be tempted to protect and preserve your position. When you are nothing, you cannot go any lower.*

"But," I exclaimed, "I said that myself, in London, in 1952!" Ten years before, when they had asked me, "Why did you resign, when you were top of the ladder, the great secretary of the World Conference?" I had told them, "If that is top of the ladder, I'm glad I got down, before I *fell* down. It's a dangerous place."

And now it suddenly came clear: If the Assemblies had not disfellowshipped me, I would never have understood what the Lord meant. But now that I had become nothing, with no position at all, I saw that I was absolutely free! With nothing to protect, I could now be all things to all men! They could not say, "You're working for the Assemblies." They could not say, "You're working for the Pentecostals." They could not say that I was working for anybody, but Jesus.

As you moved beyond your denomination, did you ever speak to the Jews?

Most of my ministry was first to the Protestants and then to the Catholics, but there were a number of occasions on which I addressed Jews. I remember one in par-

ticular, when I was invited to speak at a ministers' frater-
nal meeting in a Jewish synagogue. "Before I speak on the
Holy Spirit and Pentecost," I began, "let me first address
myself to our hosts, the Jewish Rabbis. I thank them for
inviting me, because I have learned so much; I am glad you
have kept the laws of God and the Old Testament alive for
us. We are New Testament, of course, but the Old
Testament is a rich heritage for us."

I recalled Moses going up Mt. Sinai and receiving the
law — and coming down and, when he saw what happened, he smashed the tablets which contained the Law.
And so he went back and pleaded for a duplicate. And
God obliged him. And then come this remarkable thing
that God must have said to him: "Don't destroy them
again; put them in a box." (How often have I heard
preachers say: "You can't put the Holy Spirit in a box.")
But this was what God was telling Moses: "Put them in a
box and close the lid. Don't put them up for display; the
Law is not to be displayed forever. And the lid of the box
is to be called the mercy seat." How wonderful! The Law
has now become subject to mercy! God did not intend to
rule by law, but by mercy.

You may not be able to put the Spirit in a box, but the
Spirit of God came as a flame right on the mercy seat.
Mercy will always welcome the Spirit, or manifest the
Spirit. And God had previously said: "Don't make any
images to worship." But now He said to make two images
of cherubims kneeling and facing one another, with their
wings stretched out towards each other. How beautiful!
And right between them is the shekinah glory of God,
lighting up their faces, so that they could see each other
more clearly and lovingly.

"But," I told them, "if those two fellows had had a
quarrel and turned their backs on each other, they would

not be able to see each other anymore, let alone the glory. That's why this meeting today is so wonderful! Here we are, far different from each other, but Jew and Catholic facing each other, Episcopalian and Pentecostal facing each other." I said, "Look: we're *all* facing each other, and the glory is in the midst."

I concluded by describing what the Ark of the Covenant meant to me: "It is a miracle of God's grace, recognizing the Law, and preserving the Law, but only effective if applied under the authority of mercy." I paused and smiled. "You know, I was listening to the singing of the 23rd Psalm, and when they got to 'Surely goodness and mercy shall follow me all the days of my life,' I somehow knew it was true. I happen to believe in guardian angels, and if I have two, those are their names — Goodness and Mercy."

12

PENTECOSTALS AND PROTESTANTS

The author's first steps beyond the boundaries of the Pentecostal Movement were made in the direction of first the National Council of Churches and then the World Council. In this, he was fulfilling the prophecy of Smith Wigglesworth — and also ensuring his eventual expulsion by Pentecostal brethren. But his willingness to obey God, no matter what the consequences, played a vital role in the growing move towards ecumenism. For God had indeed poured out His Spirit upon all flesh . . . .

Who is this Dr. Mackay, to whom you frequently refer?

John Alexander Mackay was president of Princeton Seminary up to his retirement. He also was president of the International Missionary Council, and president of the Reformed and Presbyterian World Alliance — he was a "presidented" man, all the way around.

We first met, when I was secretary of the Pentecostal World Conference. Naturally, I was interested in everything anybody said about us, and so I was intrigued to read the opinion of the president of Princeton Seminary, Dr. Mackay. Before his return, he had been a missionary in South America, at which time he had said that the Protestants were making headway there; in fact, "the only fly in the ointment of Protestantism are the Pentecostals." But now he was reported as saying that the greatest blessing that he found in South America was the flourishing Pentecostal Church.

Goodness me, I thought, it would be worth talking to such a man! I was living in Stamford, Connecticut, at the time, and it would not be too difficult to get down to Princeton, so I called him.

"Thank heavens you've called!" he said. "You're the kind of man I've been looking for; come along and have lunch with me, as soon as you can." So I drove down, and we talked.

"So," he said to me, "it seems you are now interested in ecumenism. For what you're doing is establishing or advancing a Pentecostal ecumenism." Instead of calling it fellowship, he called it ecumenism, and he kept using the word, until I finally asked him what it meant. For I had seen the World Council, who had employed the phrase "ecumenical council," become upset when Rome also began using that phrase.

"First they take the word 'catholicism' and make it their own, and now they take 'ecumenism'."

"Dr. Mackay, let me remind you that at one time you thought the Pentecostals were the fly in the ointment."

He nodded. "That was in the beginning; they did things that were so strange to me, a very staid Presbyterian. But since taking my post here, I've been back on a visit to the same places where I had previously lived and ministered, up and down Chile and Peru. I found that the Presbyterian Chruch still had 120 members, the same number as when I left . . . that's what I left there. And they were still singing, 'Hold the fort, for I am coming.' " He shook his head. "There'd been no progress at all."

In the course of conversation with them, he had asked them about the Pentecostal church, which had been in a shop somewhere. Did that church still exist?

"Yes," they said.

"And what are they doing?"

"They've got a church of 1,000 members now."

"What! How?"

"Well," they said, "you remember they were on a corner across from a honky-tonk?" He nodded. "They had such good noisy meetings and singing and shouting that the band leader of the honky-tonk came over to see what was going on. He got converted and gave up the band, and his band followed him. So the Pentecostals ended up with the honky-tonk's band in their church." Dr. Mackay smiled. "That's why, in South America you can hardly find a Pentecostal church anywhere that doesn't have an orchestra. I was in one that had four orchestras and four choirs. They had 1600 people, singing or playing — a big congregation all by itself!"

I knew what he was talking about; they often had congregations of four and five thousand. In Brazil, there were more Pentecostals than in the United States — several million. Indeed, Cardinal Willebrands would tell the bishops in Rome, that in South America, 80% of all non-Catholics were Pentecostal. "That," said Dr. Mackay, "was when I came to the conclusion that I would rather put up with the uncouth life of the Pentecostal, than be bound by the ascetic death of the formal churches."

I looked at him. "Dr. Mackay, this makes me feel I need you. You understand what I'm trying to do, and you're in favor of it!"

"Well," he said, "I would love to introduce you into the ecumenical movement in the churches, because you can bring them alive. Your message, your testimony — of course, I don't know you very well, but I must admit that I've never met a Pentecostal who has been in the movement so long and has come from a boy, to where he is the top man in the movement." He thought for a moment, then added, "I would like to learn more about your ministry — could you possibly come back for a week, when your schedule permits?"

I agreed, not mentioning that it was not merely a question of scheduling, but of funding. As usual, I would be entirely dependent upon the Lord for my support during that time, and as usual, He provided — in an unexpected and thrilling way. I was in a meeting in Minneapolis, speaking at the Assembly church of a father-and-son pastor team named Olsen, and I began to tell them about this new contact and the new vision that I had, not only for Pentecostal unity but for all of Christianity.

When I said that Dr. Mackay had invited me, pending my working out arrangements, the elder pastor got up and said, "What are you waiting for?"

"I have no income," I explained. "I am living on offerings and gifts."

"What will it cost you to accept this invitation?"

"At least $500, because I will have to travel from Dallas to Princeton."

"All right, we'll take an offering today, and if it's more than $500, we'll give it to you." And true to his word, that evening he turned over to me $550, for which I thanked him deeply, adding that it even took care of taxis and everything, and straight away I wrote to Dr. Mackay.

An "economical" Pentecost?

Something else happened, during that time in Minneapolis with the Olsens; I got a reputation for preaching an economical Pentecost — which, in these days of crystal cathedrals, may not be such a bad thing. How it happened was, the senior Olsen asked me, "Can you give us a topic for Sunday afternoon that will interest both Pentecostals and other churches, other ministers?"

"Very well, on Sunday afternoon I will speak about an ecumenical Pentecost."

Just before I was to follow the Olsens into the meeting, I looked out at the congregation and was surprised and delighted to see fifty to sixty ministers! And among them were a goodly number of Pentecostal ministers, whom, I assumed, had never heard of such a thing as an ecumenical Pentecost, or realized that that was what Joel meant, when he said "*all* flesh." You cannot get more ecumenical than that. And the fact is, you have *got* to be ecumenical, to be in God's eschatological plan for this age.

Two years later the Olsens invited me for a return visit, and decided to use the same topic as the previous time. When I arrived Pastor Olsen said: "Brother David, a terrible thing has happened: we put the notice in the papers, but apparently they were not familiar with the term ecumenical. Instead of printing the announcement as we gave it to them, they have announced that you will be preaching on an "Economical Pentecost." Now what do we do?"

"Well, then," I smiled, "I'm going to preach on an economical Pentecost!"

"What! Whatever will you say?"

"That's up to the Holy Spirit, and we won't know until He gives it to me. But I am still Pentecosal, and people are receiving the Baptism. I don't have to go to churches with millions of dollars of bonds, if they've got it secured, and take huge collections in my meetings. I now go to churches that are all paid for, and whose pastors are educated. They don't need anything more than the blessing of the Holy Spirit — then they can move! And brother, that's economical!"

And so I shared that, and gave another example of God's economy. Wigglesworth had said, "Empty churches will be crowded again." And how many times have Spirit-baptized pastors led small but Spirit-baptized congregations into old, empty churches? They don't cost the fortune that it would have cost to build them new, and today they are packed out. How was that for economy?

How did you become involved in the IMC?

From Minneapolis, I went to Dallas and then to Princeton, and when I arrived, Dr. 'Mackay put me in a very nice apartment and said, "This is the VIP suite. Billy Graham stays here, when he visits. I want the students to know what I think of you, and this is where faculty members can come and see you. It'll be announced."

Then he said, "The students have their own council,

and I asked them, if they would like to have a Pentecostal give a series of lectures on the Holy Spirit. They were enthusiastic, and so you are really the guest of the student body. The faculty also agreed, and so you'll have both faculty and students in your lectures."

I had a wonderful time! Recently, I re-read some of the transcripts of those lectures and was surprised at how elementary they were — my first effort to reach non-Catholics. It was Scriptural, but I did not know then the theological terminology that is understood by that type of scholar. I spoke to them, as I would speak to unlearned Pentecostals — which was undoubtedly exactly what God intended.

Dr. Mackay was pleased and kept in touch with me and I with him, of course, and as president of the Reformed & Presbyterian World Alliance, he invited me to come to San Paolo as his guest and be one of the speakers at the World Conference of the Alliance. This was a great open door, but one Presbyterian gentleman resented my coming. When he heard from missionaries whom I'd told of my invitation, he said, "I'm sure Du Plessis doesn't know what he's talking about, because I can't even get in there!" And when he arrived and found me there, registered and wearing my badge, he demanded, "How did you get in here?"

I shrugged. "I just loved my way in. I love everybody and forgive everybody, and here I am."

Not knowing I was friends with the president, he asked what I thought of Mackay.

"Oh, I think he's tops!" I said. "He's not liberal, though he will probably be accused of it, because he's so ecumenical-minded. The truth is, he's a strong believer."

Then my acquaintance confided, "The reason I can't

get in, is because I resigned from the Presbyterian World Alliance; I thought they were a worldly club."

I shook my head. "I'm afraid you've made a big blunder."

"You think I should return?"

"If I were you, I'd begin right here to re-apply."

So he asked Dr. Mackay, whether what I had said about him was true: had he said the Pentecostals were a great blessing? Dr. Mackay said, "Yes, I said so, and it is so, and Du Plessis is the champion." So, I got this man to get back into the fellowship, and then his wife went around telling people that her husband had now been led astray, back into the organized world again. And so, I learned a painful lesson: Pentecostals and Baptists are not the only ones who have difficulty with people that go independent. This is also a trait in the Protestant world. You get blessed, so get out — every time.

The Catholics are wiser in such matters. After they lost Luther, they were determined not to lose any more good men that way. What they did then was to advance "orders." Not all their orders are centuries old. When a gifted man comes along, they take him aside in the monastery and let him advance his views, his revelations, and so on. That's why you've got some wonderful orders in the Catholic Church. They don't have splits anymore — except, of course, this one man who doesn't like the liturgy in the vernacular and wants to stick with the Latin.

Incidentally, one reason why they like the Latin is that, for them, it is like our speaking in tongues. Some friends have suggested that the Gregorian Chant was originally singing in the Spirit, until they finally figured out a way to notate it and write it down. I think they are right, for I've said many times that what we call the

Heavenly Choir, singing in the Spirit, is just like the Gregorian Chant. (But I will get to the Catholics in the next chapter; right now, it's time to get back to Dr. Mackay.)

So there I was, a part of the World Alliance, and one day, as Dr. Mackay was making announcements, he said, "Our speaker for today had some attack of something and is ill in bed and cannot be here. But we have another speaker whom we're going to ask to speak to you now." As he went on to describe the next speaker, I thought, "Goodness me, he sounds like a Pentecostal, or pretty close to it; I must meet this man." And all of a sudden, he turns and says, "Now, I have not warned him; he's just sitting there, hearing about someone who is going to speak — and it's you, Dr. du Plessis. Come along now, and tell us what the Holy Spirit is doing these days." Startled, I got up and gave my message, taking great liberties, because his introduction was so favorable that nobody could think that I was a danger or a threat.

When the meeting was over, the two representatives from South Africa, one of whom was Dr. Gerdener, president of Stellenbosch Presbyterian Seminary, came up to me. "And you are a South African!" Dr. Gerdener exclaimed. "It's strange; I've been all over Europe, visiting Presbyterian or Reformed churches, and several times the name Du Plessis has come up, but I didn't know what Du Plessis they were talking about. I am going to write in the church paper in South Africa, and tell what you're doing."

But when I wrote my father that I'd met him and what he'd said, my father wrote back: "How can you be so naive! Do you really believe that these people who have persecuted us and expelled us and condemned us all the

way, will now publish something about you and what
you're doing? It can't be!"

A couple of months later, I got a cable from my father:
"A miracle has happened! Your picture and report are in
the Dutch Reformed paper." And that changed my
father's whole attitude toward the Dutch Reformed
Church, for he saw that if you approached them correctly,
you could get a hearing.

How did you become involved with the World Council of Churches?

That, too, was through Dr. Mackay. He told me that
the International Missionary Council was going to have
their final meeting in Germany in 1952, in preparation
for becoming part of the World Council. That was
ironic, for it was the missions that *brought* the World
Council into existence — Third World missionaries,
pleading for the unity of sending churches.

As I checked into that meeting in Willingen, Germany,
I recalled hearing that they had never had a Pentecostal
speaker there. Well, I thought, I probably won't get that
great a welcome; I'll just check in for three days. But at
the first coffee break, as soon as Dr. Mackay saw me, he
came over and took my arm and led me over to the line
for coffee, introducing me from the back of the line all
the way to the front, as "my great *Pentecostal* friend."

I whispered to him, "If the word Pentecostal scares
these people, you'd better use some other word, like just
Christian or evangelical."

"No," he smiled, "The truth they must hear."

And the strange thing was, every one of them said,
"Oh, so glad you're here. Can I have a little interview

with you?" I had interviews with 110 of the 210 delegates, and some of them became "Charismatic" (as we call it now) as a result.

After the first few days, the secretary of the World Council, who was attending the conference because the IMC was going to combine with the WCC, found me and said, "Do you realize that you are the most important man in this meeting?"

"Now listen," I scolded him, "you're a Hollander, not an American; don't exaggerate like that!"

"I'm not exaggerating at all. This morning in the convening circle, they said 'What has happened here? No Pentecostal has ever been here, and now one's here, and everybody's talking Pentecost, Pentecost, Pentecost! What is the matter with us?' So now," he added, chuckling, "I want you to be sure to come to the second assembly, in Evanston, two years from now, in 1954."

I accepted, and in the meantime, I refused to let my name be put forward to go on as secretary of the Pentecostal World Conference. This was in 1952. The next World Conference was in 1955, in Stockholm, and it just wasn't the same, so they said, "Let us bring Du Plessis back again. The man has done the whole thing." And that's how I was reinstated. I arranged the 1958 meeting in Toronto, and that really was my last. By that time, the executives of the Pentecostal Movement had formed the core committee, and I had become so ecumenical, they really didn't want me, even as a member.

But in response to the secretary's invitation to the WCC meeting in '54, I said, "How can I get in there? I'm not the executive of any church. I am not even a pastor. I have no legal position in the church, except I am a wandering preacher or lecturer."

"What are you basically doing now?"

"I'm working with the Far East Broadcasting Company." That turned out to be the key, for the Far East Broadcasting Company needed to make contacts with *all* Christian missions, in order to carry on and not be solely dependent upon Pentecostal support. I arranged for them to have a representative at the Evanston conference, and as a result, the World Council of Churches began to support them. I told Far East Broadcasting, "If you want to reach all nations, you're going to need all denominations."

Bishop Kennedy, the chairman of the press staff at the 1954 WCC conference in Evanston, said: "We're very fortunate to have a man like Du Plessis here. He's not afraid of foreigners, and he speaks other languages." Then he looked at me and asked, "That is right, isn't it? You do speak several other languages?"

I laughed. "With my head, very few; but with my heart, all of them."

"Oh!" he exclaimed, "the man isn't even touchy about it!" Then he added: "You're not afraid of strangers, then?"

"No."

"Then your assignment shall be to round up all the non-English speaking delegates and bring them to where we can have them recognized."

And that was how the Lord acquainted me with the whole room and opened the door for me to go anywhere in the world. I could go to any capital city and call up the bishop or archbishop, or whomever they had sent there, and could count on being welcomed with open arms. It gave me endless opportunities to minister personally to priests and missionaries everywhere.

In the speech they asked me to make, I told them, "I am not here to ask any favors or to ask recognition. I'm not even here to try to persuade you to accept Pentecost, or accept tongues. Which may seem peculiar, because the Charismatic Movement began as a tongues movement. In the early days they accused us of being a tongues movement and used the term as an insult. But today I say the tongues movement did not begin at Pentecost; it began with the Tower of Babel. But the same phenomenon which divided at Babel, now unites in Pentecost. For the Spirit is ecumenical: He is the all-flesh Spirit poured out upon all flesh. And that means that He will do what Jesus said: 'When He comes, He will reprove the world of sin.' "

I laughed. "And here, we've considered it *our* duty to attack the world and call them sinners. What *we* ought to concentrate on is salvation and healing and forgiveness. That's why I do not often use the word 'sinners,' or 'devil.' 'But, David,' they say, 'you must speak the truth.' 'I do,' I answer them, 'but I leave the reproving to the Holy Spirit. When I speak to them about forgiveness, the Holy Spirit is there to show them the way. He wants to make you an heir of God, and joint heirs with Christ, if you accept His forgiveness.' "

Has your association with the WCC had any direct benefit?

Soon after I joined, I was approached by Bill Wilson, the secretary of the Elim Mission Churches, and one of our most effective African missionaries. Bill was on the horns of a dilemma. "We're having great difficulty getting into Kenya and other African territories. They won't let us in. We were advised to join the National Association of Evangelicals, and have them apply for us, and at first, they promised us they would fix everything, and in no time we'd be recognized. But they wound up rejecting us, because we are a conglomeration — a fellowship of independent churches. So, we can't get any help from them."

It was a predicament, all right; I knew that even if the NAE dared recognize them, the missionaries out in those territories would not recognize them. They would be left having to work with the Pentecostals, who had their hands full with their own missions. So now what?

"Well," Bill went on, "we prayed, and there came a prophecy: do not be discouraged; the Lord will make a way. If you go to David du Plessis, he will show you that way." And he looked at me, expectantly.

"Bill, the only way that I can show you is the World Council, specifically their International Missionary Council. I know the men on the Council, and I know their secretary. I can talk to them, but I can't guarantee —"

"I don't care what it is," he cut in, "the Lord is evidently in favor of it, or He wouldn't have had us come to you."

I called Dr. Mackay then, and told him about Elim's plight. "I'm calling you," I said, "instead of the secretary whom I don't know so well. But you know him."

Dr. Mackay thought for a moment. "All right, I'll tell you what: I'll call him and tell him to give you all the assistance possible."

The secretary was an Englishman, stationed in New York, and so I went to see him. It seemed that he knew me better than I knew him. "Oh," he said, "you are recognized among us, as if you'd always belonged, because you act like you are really ecumenical."

"Well, what can I do for my friends?"

"Tell them to explain their whole position in a letter to you. Then make a copy of that letter and send it to me,

with a letter of your own, and I'll take care of the rest."
When I had done as he instructed, he sent Elim's letter
and my letter with one of his own, to their headquarters
in England (at that time Britain still maintained a
presence in East Africa, in Kenya). They, in turn,
informed the government in Kenya, that these people
were indeed worthy and had the approval of top Pentecostal leaders. They must be given the freedom to open
up schools and churches.

To Elim's surprise, they not only got permission to
open up the schools that they had applied for, but they
were given a whole list of other schools that needed
supervision, and that was where they began to thrive.
They got T. L. Osborn to come out there and were able
to set up meetings for him that drew the biggest crowds
anybody had ever known. And that was how Osborn
became an international figure. Today that movement is
stronger than the rest of the Pentecostals, because Joseph
Mattsson-Boze and Charles Weston went out there and
held seminars for uneducated leaders. They told them, in
effect, that they didn't have to be formally educated to be
in leadership; if God had called them to establish a work,
He would give them the wisdom they needed. They
taught them themselves and gave them a bicycle and a
P.A. system (the sum total of their equipment) and sent
them out.

Recently I saw Joseph Mattsson-Boze, who told me
that afterwards one of their students had gotten fully
educated by correspondence schools, and was today a
great leader in Zaire. But at the time, he was giving the
basics to as many as he could, and also attempting to line
up some refresher courses for those already pastoring.
"How many can you feed?" Joseph asked them.

"We haven't got the funds," they told him.

"Well, I will try to get you between $500 and $1,000 to feed pastors. Getting here will be their own problem; they can walk, if necessary. But we must be able to feed them." And so this was our next request to the World Council. The point is, the evangelicals didn't even want to accept them into their fellowship, and were not prepared to help them in this way. The World Council has more official influence, for the only major body that's not in the World Council are the Catholics. The Orthodox and Greek Orthodox and Russian Orthodox are all in the World Council. So, this ecumenical bent of mine has indeed had tremendous, tangible advantages.

But it was all prophesied beforehand, by Smith Wigglesworth, who said that I must talk to the leaders from the top, and when I attended the meeting in '52, I was speaking to the top Protestant representatives from the mission field, from the Third World — it's a strange thing, how much has come out of the Third World.

Regarding Christianity, what lies ahead for the Third World?

I say the future of Christianity lies in the Third World, not in the old world. The old world needs much repentance and renewal and so on, but the Third World is getting it all fresh. And they're coming in by the millions! Incidentally, the greatest danger to Third World Christianity comes not from Communism, but from Islam.

The Moslems are trying to capture Africa, and to a large extent you'll find them accepted, because with Islam, the Africans just change a few names, and they are all right. There is no call for conversion, or the total commitment that Christianity requires. The Moslems have only the Koran. Yet they do make a difference, because they do have some form of holiness and spirituality. In fact, I have been in some Moslem countries where they act more like Christians, than sometimes Christians themselves do. And, remember, they have eight hundred million people praying, five times a day. How many Christians pray that often?

But we are making inroads. In the strongest Moslem city in Nigeria, they told the German missionary evangelist Reinhard Bonnke, that he would make no headway there at all. But he worked with the black Nigerian prelate, Archbishop Benson Idahosa, and according to the police, he had an audience of half a million.

Wigglesworth had always said that speaking was necessary for miracles. And now Bonnke confided: "Brother David, God said to me: *If you speak the Word under the unction, under the anointing of the Holy Spirit, you are speaking just as if I myself were speaking. You are an ambassador. Speak the Word!* And so, Bonnke would challenge them. He would ask if any of them had come on crutches, and he would say, "In Jesus' name, take your healing, throw down your crutches, and come up here." And they saw a man with crutches in his hands running down the center aisle. And all the people in the meeting would see him. You can imagine what effect that would have on them! Miracles have a place, but they must be attributed not to the man, but to Jesus, and Bonnke knew that. "I must always say," he told me, "that I speak for Jesus, and I speak in His name."

How do you feel about things back in America?

Back home, the trend towards super-churches seems to be growing stronger. Here you have a conference for pastors who have more than a thousand in Sunday School, and another for pastors with 2,500 or more — I was the keynote speaker at the first meeting of one such conference a couple of years ago, and as often happens with me, I had little advance notice. The chairman said, "There you are! I've been looking all over for you; where have you been?"

"Seeing my son off at the airport."

"I've made up my mind that you are to be our speaker; you go on in ten minutes."

"Is that fair?"

"Well, I know that to ask anyone else would have been useless, but you are always ready." So, I agreed, on the condition that we leave the subject to the Lord, and let Him guide me.

But now I needed a subject. I prayed, and the Lord seemed to say: *Speak on the seven churches of Revelation.* So I did. "I want to speak to you this morning about a Scriptural pattern. I have heard you pastors talking at this conference, comparing notes, sharing techniques on how to build your congregations even larger. And this morning the Lord brought to mind the Book of Revelation. In it, the Lord Jesus, the Head of the Church, appoints John His secretary, and dictates a letter to him, to the seven different churches. Now it is not the same letter, to be distributed to all the churches; it is a different letter for each church. And to whom does He have John address each letter? To the angel of each church — in other words, its pastor."

I looked around, and they were surprisingly attentive for a morning audience. "But note: He did not address each letter to the angel of the church *and* the elders, or the board. He held the angel of the church totally responsible for the merits and demerits of that church. You pastors are forming boards of elders, and now you say you want to have 'Body Ministry.' No matter what you have, Jesus is going to hold each of you personally responsible for what goes on in your church."

They were even more attentive now. "And I'll tell you something else: He did not say to one church, 'You go learn from the other.' He did not tell Ephesus to go to Philadelphia, or tell Philadelphia, 'Why don't you do like Ephesus?' He never drew comparisons. Each of your churches has its own unique character, its own traditions. You all are behaving like a bunch of copy-cats! You sit here, you hear what another man does, and you make notes; you're going to introduce that in your city, as soon as you get home. But according to Revelation, what Jesus said was good for one church, was *not* good for another. It will lead you into wrong practices."

They knew what I meant. There were churches there with two or three thousand people in their Sunday Schools — because their pastors had announced that the recruiter who bussed in the most people four weeks in a row would win a free refrigerator. "That," I said, "is *not* the Holy Spirit." They got the message. They may not have liked it, but they got it.

Sadly, the thing they didn't seem to realize is that in this era the Holy Spirit is not working as He did before. No longer depending on the Church alone, He is now moving ahead of the Church. For example, what is *not* happening in Europe, the most churchified of all nations, is a tragedy. But now, by means of television, the Spirit is moving beyond the churches and into the homes.

By contrast, look at what *is* happening in nations that have not even got a testimony of Jesus: there you have what I call national renewals. As I've said, there is where you also have a strong Moslem influx, for they are the greatest opposition to nations becoming Christianized.

When I look at the revival in Indonesia, there I see that the Church is doing something wise. There, and in India, they are now sending in ex-Moslems, to evangelize the Moslems. And they are having far more success than foreign Christian missionaries ever used to.

But the harvest time is passing quickly — too quickly, for there has not been the teaching that this anointing, this outpouring of the Spirit, is for *ministry*, nothing else. When Joel specified "sons and daughters, servants and handmaidens," he was referring to the *laity*, the general public. That is why I encourage youth and labor to minister, and encourage pastors to recognize everybody as part of the royal priesthood. Too many pastors are still trying to do the whole job themselves. "That's why you all get heart attacks," I tell them. "You should take it easy and be leaders, not drivers." There's too much driving.

So that is why I say that the Pentecost of the future lies not in the renewal of the churches; it lies in the renewal of nations.

13

PENTECOSTALS AND CATHOLICS

In 1949, the author was appointed General Secretary to the Pentecostal World Conference, and as such was perhaps the most influential leader in the movement. But God had other work for him to do — work that would take him far from confines of his denomination. The leadership of the denomination could not understand, but he had no choice but to obey God. First, he reached out to the Protestants, and then to the Catholics, and when he refused to desist, he was disfellowshipped. There is no bitterness on his part, but he has a unique perspective on — and definition of — ecumenism.

By the Lord's appointment, I have been the one that ventured out of the Pentecostal Movement in 1952. You see, I grew up in a Pentecostal hot-house. We kept the temperature right, and thought everybody outside was either freezing or burning up. And then the Lord told me to get out of that isolation, segregation, separation — even insulation — and see what He had been doing. I got outside — and I found it was spring-time! The desert was blooming, the churches were changing and were ready for the Holy Spirit. And so now, I will not allow anybody to coop me up in any kind of limited ministry.

There is this wonderful thought that we call ecumenical. Of course, I had all my life known what a good word "catholic" was. And I have always been catholic — universal, not Roman Catholic. My brother always says, "If you speak about the Catholic Church with the Vatican in Rome, call it Roman Catholic." The rest of it is catholic — a thing that as a Pentecostal I was about to learn.

How did you happen to go to the Catholics?

I did not want to go to the Catholics. I still had my Pentecostal objections — it was a false church, and what could I do? I did have one warning, when I was preaching one day in the Angelus Temple, headquarters of the Foursquare Gospel Church, founded by Amy Mac-Pherson in Echo Park, Los Angeles. There, a brother came up to me afterwards and said: "You mention the World Council and the National Council, you tell about all the things God is doing in the Protestant world, but you never mention the Catholics."

I shook my head. "I don't know about the Catholics. Frankly, I don't want anything to do with them."

"But I saw a vision! In it, you were standing before a whole lot of cardinals in red robes, and you were speaking to them."

"Oh," I said, "I'll take the warning, but the Lord will have to do a miracle." Little did I know . . .

Not long after, in Greenville, South Carolina, I met Cameron Townsend, founder of the Wycliffe Bible Translators, and he knew of what I was doing. "You must go to Rome," he said. "Pope John will soon be convening a Vatican Council, and you should be there."

"What do you mean: I must go?"

"I'll get a hundred and fifty thousand signatures, to send you as our delegate."

"Sir, I won't go, if you get a million and a half signatures!"

"You won't go?"

"No, not this way."

"Well, how would you go?"

"If they invite me."

"How do you expect to get an invitation?"

"I don't know. But if I'm to go, the Lord will work one out. I go nowhere, unless I'm invited."

What changed your attitude about going?

Karl Barth. He said to me: "Have you ever given the Catholics a thought?"

"No," I replied, "but I have had several warnings that the Lord might want me to go to the Catholics. Needless to say, I am not anxious for that at all."

"Listen to me!" he said strongly. "You are excited about what has happened in the World Council. Well, I was the keynote speaker in Amsterdam, and I have no hope that the World Council will ever bring unity in Christianity. But when God moves the Catholic Church, you ought to be on the scene."

"You really think so?"

He nodded. "The Holy Father is a friend of mine, and I know the vision he has for the renewal of the Church." He paused, then added, "The door will be open soon, and when it is, you must go to Rome."

I knew of his friendship with John XXIII; in fact, there was an apocryphal story about it. Someone asked Pope John, whom he considered the greatest theologian in the Protestant world.

"I'm not supposed to judge people," he is reputed to have said, "but in this instance it's not for publication: I am convinced the greatest theologian I know is Karl Barth."

When this was reported to Barth, he replied, "Well, so the Holy Father is infallible, after all!"

What happened then?

I waited, and meanwhile I was invited to Edinburgh, Scotland, to speak to the Commission of Faith and Order of the World Council, prior to going to New Delhi. I spoke on faith and order, and then challenged them: "Why have your churches perpetuated water baptism, and yet you have made no provision for Jesus to be the Baptizer in the Holy Spirit? I know you still acknowledge Him as the Saviour, but John, who introduced Him as 'the Lamb of God who takes away the sin of the world,' also said, 'He'll baptize you in the Holy Ghost.' Why do you accept the first and not the second? My challenge to you tonight is: what will you do with Jesus, if you don't make provison for Him to meet the Church, the same way as He began in Jerusalem, when they turned the world upside-down?"

Afterwards, when the people came up, here came a man in a black suit and round collar who put his arm around me. "Will you also accept the sincere thanks and deep gratitude of a Catholic priest?"

I said, "Who are you?"

"Oh, I'm Bernard Leaming from Oxford, and I've been sent here as an observer by Pope John. But now I've learned something from you that I didn't know. I've been a priest for 40 years, and in Rome for 11 of them, and I've never heard anyone call Jesus the Baptizer."

"Well," I said, "that was the way the Lord told me to approach it, for a man like yourself." I smiled. "It's in the Bible; you can look it up." He asked if he could have breakfast with me, and I said, "All right, if I get in first, I'll turn a chair for you, and if you get in first, you turn one for me."

The next morning, I asked him: "Did you sleep well?"

"I couldn't sleep at all."

"Did what I say disturb you?"

"It certainly did. I tried to find the word 'baptizer' in the concordance, but I couldn't. I did find 'baptize' — 'I baptize in water; He'll baptize in the Holy Spirit.' And then I came to John's gospel, 1:33, 'He that sent me to baptize in water, the same said to me: the one upon whom you see the Spirit descend and remain upon him, he is the baptizer in the Holy Spirit.' " He paused. "I was going to correct your theology, but here I found you were right. I went on to Acts 1, where Jesus says, 'you shall be baptized in the Holy Spirit.' I saw that He had *commanded* them not to depart from Jerusalem, until they had received what He called 'the promise of the Father.' And I thought, 'Oh, he's got the Father on his side, and now he's got the Son, too!' And then I came to Peter saying, 'Jesus says the Spirit will remind you what I taught you.' " He looked at me. "David — can I call you David?"

I smiled. "That's what my friends call me."

"Well, I want to be your friend. David, you have the authority of Father, Son, and Holy Ghost, that this baptism is what happened at Pentecost."

I said gently: "You have perpetuated water baptism and called it John's baptism. Why did you not perpetuate the baptism of Jesus?"

He nodded. "It should have happened all through the ages, but didn't. So much of it has disappeared . . ." and he sighed and looked out the window. "All these years, I've never realized that this is the ministry of Jesus." Now he turned back. "You know, that must be true for many others. I'm sure the Holy Father doesn't know it, either," he chuckled. "You'll have to go to Rome to tell him."

"Well," I smiled, "Carson Blake has invited me to the World Council meetings in New Delhi. Perhaps I will stop in Rome on the way back and see what happens." But I had no idea that he would write to Rome, in advance of my visit, telling them that he had met a man full of the Holy Ghost and full of love.

What happened in Rome?

When I arrived at Rome's Fumicino airport, I looked around for the Pentecostals who usually met me, but they were nowhere to be seen. I found out why later, when I called the office of the Assembly of God church there, to see if there was any mail. As sometimes happened, I had run totally out of money, and had to call Anna, to ask her to send me some.

Yes, they said, the letter was there, and then they

added, "There are Catholic priests all over the place, looking for you. Are you in trouble?"

"Not me," I said, "they are. What's their trouble?"

"They want to know about the Holy Spirit."

"Did anyone leave a phone number?"

"Yes, there was a Dr. Murray here, a British priest, and he left his number."

"Give it to me."

So I called Dr. Murray, and he said to me, "Now that I know where you are, can I see you? We have heard that you are a man full of the Holy Ghost and full of love. Such a man I want to meet, and the sooner the better."

"How soon is sooner?"

"I can be there in twenty minutes."

"Well," I said, "I've got nothing else to do; come along."

I put the phone down, and I said, "Lord, now I'm really in trouble! This man expects love, and I've never loved a Catholic! Lord, You've changed me towards the Protestants; You helped me to forgive them and love them. Please, do it once more. And Lord, You'd better hurry; You've only got twenty minutes!"

When the knock came at the door, I opened it, and this priest threw out his arms, grabbed ahold of me, and embraced me, and putting his head on my shoulder, he said: "Thank God that I've met you! I need your prayers."

And I said, "Father Murray, I need yours just as badly." And a strange thing happened: we wept together. And I found that I loved this man. From then on, I loved Catholics, all of them. I forgave every one, right up to the Pope himself. Because the Lord said, *If you don't forgive, you cannot love, and if you don't love, I can't use you.*

And so, this blessed man took me around to see all the great cardinals and heads of colleges, and after a few days he shook his head and said, "I must admit, you truly are led of the Spirit."

"What makes you say that?"

"Because you never ask, 'How do I behave? What do I do here or there?' You always do the right thing."

I did not know quite how to reply to that. "Well," I said, "I'm under the anointing for ministry, and the Lord knows what I need."

"That must be it," he said, still mystified. "Because that last archbishop is an absolute terror; we're all dead scared of him, and there I was, trembling in my shoes, as we sat waiting to see him. And when he walked in, you stood up and smiled, shook hands with him, as if you'd found an old lost friend, and I saw him smile for the first time. Remarkable! You had influence on the man immediately."

"Well," I said mischievously, "I guess you might say that, being under the unction of the Holy Spirit, I am supernaturally natural," and we both laughed.

As I met more and more of these men, word got around, and we learned that Cardinal Bea wanted to see me. The first thing he asked was: "What do Pentecostals want to say to Rome?"

"Cardinal, I'm sorry, but they don't want to talk to Rome at all. And what they say about you, I'd hate to tell you."

"What do *you* want to say to Rome?"

What to say? I prayed, and an unexpected Scripture came to mind: "I'd rather speak five words with understanding, than ten thousand words in a tongue." I took that to mean it was no use praying in tongues (I called it "telephoning to glory"); I would have to speak a word of wisdom. How? I couldn't think; I had no time. But I heard myself say: "Cardinal, I have come, humbly, to beg of you and the Council, if possible, to change the order of things and liberate the Bible and make it available to all Catholics, everywhere in the world, in their own language. If Catholics will read the Bible, then Pope John's prayer for the renewal of the Church will be answered. That will change the Church. It will change the people, and it's the body that needs to be changed, not the Pope or the Cardinals. It doesn't need new officers, or new organization — only the Word of God is the basis for Renewal."

Cardinal Bea thumped his desk and turned to his secretary, Monsignor Schmitt: "Write that down. We'll tell the Holy Father what this holy man says."

The Wycliffe Translators believe that that is how the Lord changed things so that they are enjoying the full cooperation of all Catholic linguists in translation of the Scriptures. As it happens, many of these Catholic linguists are Charismatic, and that alarmed the Wycliffe folks, but they soon found out that people who are baptized in the Holy Spirit and speak in tongues are more comfortable with new languages and are thus able to translate much easier and much sooner. Up to his death, Uncle Cam rejoiced that the Lord had answered my prayer.

Did the invitation finally come?

In September, 1964, I received this letter from Cardinal Bea:

Dear Dr. du Plessis:

As President of the Secretariat for Promoting Christian Unity, I have the honor to invite you to attend the third session of the Second Vatican Council as a guest of the Secretariat. Although you are invited under private title, I assure you that you will enjoy the same rights and facility at the Council, as do the delegated observers. By the gesture of our invitation and your acceptance, we pray that through the Holy Spirit, your presence as a guest will be an efficacious contribution to an ever-increasing understanding and esteem between all those who believe in Christ, our common Lord and Master.

Prayerfully united in fidelity to the Lord Jesus Christ, in His Spirit,

Augustine, Cardinal Bea

That was the letter I received; I don't think a Pentecostal could write a better one.

So now I prayed: "Lord, am I to accept this invitation to the Vatican Council?" And the Lord said, *If, before you go, you can be sure that you have forgiven them — completely, even for their history that you always mention.*

"All right, Lord, I will."

I am the God of history. Your responsibility does not go into the past; it lies in the future. I can go into the past, but you cannot.

I accepted the invitation, and that was how I was issued a Vatican passport, signed by the Cardinal himself. I had to show it a few times to get in, but I was shown to a seat right in the front row.

From the beginning, I was sure the Holy Spirit had arranged this meeting, and the Holy Spirit was moving, and so I sat there from day to day, early and late. When I saw those cardinals get up, I knew the coffee bar was open, so I would walk there and look around and pray, Lord, guide me, help me. Then I would look at a fellow and think, I like his face; I'll go and stand beside him, so that when he turns round with his coffee or his soda, he'll bump me. And if he bumps me, I will, of course, apologize. So I did.

"I'm sorry," I said, "I got in your way."

"Oh! you speak English?"

"Yes, sir."

"Where do you come from?"

"California."

"Oh? You're a long ways from home."

"Yes, but I'm quite happy here."

"What is your name?"

"David du Plessis."

"Ah! You're the Pentecostal."

"Yes, sir."

"Hah. You mean, you've got the Pentecostal experience."

"Yes."

"Are you coming to tell us we can get it, too?"

"Yes."

"And when we get it, must we talk in tongues?"

"No. You must *not* — but you *will*."

And that is how I made friends with so many of them. When the Dutch fellows found out I was there, one day I had a whole ring of them around me, and again the Lord helped me. One bishop said to me: "I have heard that you have no objections to Mary."

I looked at him in astonishment. "How could I? She's the mother of my Lord. How could I expect Jesus to approve of my ministry, if I didn't like His mother?" The bishops surrounding us roared with laughter.

"But do you pay any attention to Mary?"

"Sir, I'd have you know that every day of my life, from early morning till late at night, I do what Mary said. I never do anything except what Mary says."

He looked at me, his eyes widening. "What does she say?"

"She always says to me: 'What He says, do it.' " And I paused and looked at him: "Do *you* do what Mary says?"

"What do you mean?"

"I mean, do you do everything Jesus says?"

"No, I can't say I do."

"Then you'd better get started; Mary's going to be awfully mad at you if you don't."

So, here in that Council comes a suggestion that Mary should be called Mother of the Church. You should have heard the arguments! I never thought such a distinguished crowd would get so hot under the collar!

Finally, one old cardinal from Mexico stood up and said, "I have never worshipped Mary. I reverence her, and I love her. But I don't worship her, and I don't like this. I've been taught from my childhood that the Church is my mother, God is the Father, and if you now make Mary Mother of the Church, that will make her my grandmother!" Half the bishops roared with laughter; the other half gnashed their teeth.

I knew the Council was divided, and I prayed: "O Lord, don't let this Council split on this issue." The matter went to Pope Paul, and he sent back notice that the argument must stop; Mary may be called Mother of the Church.

So, here they come into the coffee bar, and I am the only Pentecostal there; I have got to answer for everything. "David," said one bishop, "you know that the Holy Father has decided Mary may be called Mother of the Church. Do you have any objections?"

"None at all."

"Can you accept Mary as Mother of the Chruch?"

"Well, my only difficulty is that it's a little premature."

"You cannot accept Mary?"

"Not yet."

"But you think some day you will?"

"Yes, I'm sure one day I'll have to."

"Why?"

"Well, have you never read of the Marriage Supper of the Lamb? Jesus was the bridegroom; who was the bride?"

"The Church."

I nodded. "After the Bridegroom, Jesus, is united with the Church, all throughout history, Mary will be the mother-in-law of the Church."

He laughed and said: "That sounds reasonable. It may not be good theology, but it's perfect logic."

(Isn't it wonderful how, when you love people, you can find excuses for them, if you want to?) I went on: "But I also know that I was still courting my wife, when I began to call her mother, Mother — before we were married. So, I'm going to do the same with Mary — she's Mother."

I was preaching in this vein one night in Bangalore, to some ten thousand people. Mother Teresa was sitting there, and with her was the cardinal who was Charismatic, and eight bishops. Once again I said: "I have no objections to you having such a regard for Mary, on the condition that you do what she says — 'Whatsoever He says, do it.' She does not give orders at all. She

ended her ministry to Him, when she handed Him over
and said, 'Whatsoever he says, do it.' If you love Mary,
you'll do what she says; if you do, you can expect her Son
to perform miracles in your church."

And then I added: "What He says won't always be
what you expect. The problem at that wedding in Cana
was wine, but instead of telling them where to find wine,
He never even mentioned it. He told them to fetch
water."

I imagined what my reaction would have been, had I
been one of the servants there: "Lord, did you hear what
your mother said? Water is not relevant to the solution of
this problem."

"But," He'd say to me, "if you do what I say, I'm going
to turn that water into wine."

"Well, please don't put it in stone pots! That's not
traditional; it's supposed to go in leather bags." You see,
everything He said was wrong.

Is it true that you prophesied the election
of John Paul II?

Not exactly. I was in Europe, when I received a cable
that John Paul I had passed away, after serving as Holy
Father for only 33 days, as the successor to Paul VI. In
the triangle between Germany, France, and Switzerland,
there is a Catholic church, and I spoke with its priest,
who said, "You know, they are electing a new Pope right
now."

"Yes," I nodded, "I'm praying for them right now. At
the Vatican Council, we were told: 'Jesus is the Head of
the Church,' and that's whom I'm talking to."

"Have you got any idea of what's going to happen?"

"I've got an idea," I smiled, "but I can't say that the Lord has told me so."

"What's your idea?"

"That this time God is going to make a change, and it's not going to be an Italian."

"Not an Italian?"

"No," I said, "They've been there 406 years, and that rut is just like an old grave, with both ends knocked out. It's dead! God wants to bring new life."

The priest made a note on his pad. "And what nationality will he be?"

"I don't know; again, God didn't tell me anything. But I have an idea..."

He clapped his hands. "You must share this in the church tonight, as we gather to pray for the deliberations in the Vatican."

That night, as I spoke from the platform, the people prayed fervently, and some sobbed and cried out, "Lord we want the renewal of the Chruch, however You want to do it! We pray that Your will be done for this election down in Italy."

The following night I was in Winterthur, for a pre-arranged meeting in the French Reformed Church. As I came in, just before the meeting, who should come up but another priest friend. Greeting him, I said, "I'm very happy to see you here! I didn't think you would come to a French Reformed Church."

"I'll go anywhere, if David du Plessis's the speaker!" he laughed. "Besides, my whole congregation is here. They've heard that you prophesied last night that the next Pope will not be an Italian."

"Good grief, who told you that?"

"David, after you finished that meeting last night, that priest sat at that phone and called all the priests in

Switzerland and told them to pray — David says it will
not be an Italian." He laughed again, and I smiled weakly.
Then he added: "Please repeat that from the platform
tonight. Say it again. I want my people to hear it,
because if there is a change, it will echo throughout the
world." So I agreed.

I started off by recalling the process of *aggiornismento*
— the throwing open of the window to let the fresh air in
— begun by John XXIII, when he convened the Vatican
Council. "He could not complete it," I told them. "Paul
followed him, and I knew Paul best of all and am convinced that he was both born again and baptized in the
Spirit. He was a man after my heart, and now he's gone.
And I knew the Patriarch of Venice, from an afternoon
spent in dialogue with him in that city. He was a saint, but
a sickly man, and I was surprised when I heard that he had
accepted the position. Still, I thought he was the right
man. He took the name of John Paul I and did not have
time to finish what John XXIII had begun. If the man
who is now to become Pope is wise, he will take the name
of John Paul II."

That was Sunday night. On Monday morning, the
newspapers announced that the new Pope was a Polish
cardinal from Cracow, who had taken the name John
Paul II.

Is the last obstacle to unity, the Catholics' separate communion?

If not the last, certainly it is one of the last. While
praying about it, I seemed to hear the Lord say, *You are
the best-known Pentecostal in the world. Suenens is the
best-known Catholic leader in the Charismatic Movement. And yet you two cannot sit together around the*

Table of the Lord. With this attitude, you are bringing judgment upon the Body of Christ. This is the Body that is suffering, because you, as leaders, are not in the place where you can give the example to the whole Chruch. You teach John 17 in vain, because the unity that was prayed for at the First Eucharist, will eventually have to come around the Table of the Lord.

Until his recent retirement, Cardinal Suenens, the first cardinal to openly admit that he had spoken in tongues, was the liaison between the Pope and the Charismatic Movement. And with the burden for a common table heavy on my heart, the next time I was in Brussels, I made an appointment to see my old friend. At that date, he was in the middle of a conference of Catholic Charismatic leaders in Europe and had to postpone the agreed-upon hour.

When he came out of the meeting, he took me by the arm and said, "Come with me," and we went into a private room. Closing the door, he turned to me and smiled. "Every time we speak, you seem to have a fresh revelation. Well, today, my friend, I *need* something fresh from the Lord."

Startled, I silently thanked God for having just opened the door for something that had been weighing deeply on my heart. "I do have a fresh revelation for you, and for myself, as well. I am called Mr. Pentecost, and seem to be the liaison between everybody, and you are the liaison between the Holy Father and the Charismatic Movement. We love each other, yet we cannot sit at the table of the Lord together."

He stared at me, without saying a word, and I went on. "The Lord now tells me that for two of his servants — to each of whom He has entrusted so much — to be divided at His table is tantamount to eating and drinking damnation upon His Body — upon the Church."

He never took his eyes from mine, as the silence between us lengthened. At last, he said, "Only God could teach you that! If you had come one hour earlier today, I wouldn't have understood what you are saying. And if you had come one hour later, it would be too late. This is the hour."

Without explaining further, he got up and said, "Lunch is ready, come along." At lunch with us was a psychiatrist and his wife, and a wonderfully charismatic professor whom I didn't know, who was to speak at their conference later that day, on behalf of Killian McDonnell, who had taken ill. All at once, the Cardinal turned to me and said, "Now, will you repeat what you have just told me back there." I looked at him, nonplussed. "Tell them," he assured me, "I want them to hear it." And so I did.

When I finished, he said to them, "I must admit, it's a thought that I have never had. But it has made such an impression on me that I can see we will have to begin to pray. At least in *my* heart, I am absolutely prepared to sit down at the Lord's Table any time with David du Plessis, and with others, but I still have a church that will not agree to this, and they are not all charismatic, either." It was then that I learned that the whole morning they had been struggling with this question of open Communion, and could not get an answer. They did not know where to go.

I stayed to hear the professor read Killian McDonnell's prepared paper — in which he cited the prayer that Jesus prayed at the table, that they all may be one (John 17:21), and made his appeal there. When the professor finished reading, he said, "David is here. We have not asked him to speak to us, but he has spoken to the Cardinal, and if the Cardinal approves, I will tell you what he said." He looked at Cardinal Suenens, who nodded, and he related the whole story. The meeting broke into tears and prayed, "Lord, make us one."

After that, often whenever I was invited to speak to Catholic audiences, with the permission of my host, I would close with that appeal. One time, John Bertolucci was the chairman of a meeting where I spoke to 600 (a thousand more had to be turned away for lack of room). As I concluded, many got down on the floor and lay on their faces before the Lord, and John Bertolucci was one. Sobbing like a baby, he cried out to the Lord, for unity of God's people around His table.

Do you think there will be a change soon?

I don't know. A few of the Catholic Charismatic leadership are guardedly optimistic, pointing out the strides that have been made since 1967, when the Catholics became involved in the Charismatic Movement — advances they believe are a result of their ongoing prayers and patience.

But I would have to say that the majority of leadership is expressing, in varying degrees, concern about the forthcoming synod — that it might decide that the Charismatic Movement has moved away from the traditional, the old Catholic tradition. As a result, there has been a subtle but distinct dampening of the influence of the Charismatic Movement.

Incidentally, something similar is happening in the Anglican Chruch. The Archbishop of Canterbury told me that he was praying for the Charismatic Renewal to pass away, in order that the whole Church would become Charismatic. So I caution my Anglican friends, and my Catholic friends, too: be grateful that you are tolerated and do not push for official recognition. Because if you get official recognition, you also get official control. Leave it be, and thank God for tolerance. For if they will tolerate it, the leaven can work, and there will be no controlling it.

Will the erosion of the Charismatic influence among Catholics continue?

I don't know that, either. At their leadership conference, Kevin Ranaghan told them how concerned he was that prayer groups of three, four, and five hundred people had, over the years, been reduced to 30, 40 and less, and the biggest of all was no longer even operating. I told Kevin that the reason these great Charismatic fellowships had gone down, was because some men in authority were insisting that they be 100% Catholic, no outsiders. "Look," I said to him, "that Bishops' Conference in 1969 decided that bishops must appoint prudent priests to act as liaison between them and the prayer groups, and the bishops appointed priests who were baptized in the Holy Spirit. But then they also had their organization, and in that organization were men who headed up the matter of liturgy and worship. And those fellows said, 'Why must they have a special liaison? They ought to come under my jurisdiction.' And that was the beginning of the end."

Kevin then recalled my coming to their fellowship in South Bend, back when they had only been going for two years and saying: "This is a spontaneous move of the Holy Spirit; *don't organize it.*"

Recalling the glory of those early days, we were both sad. I said to Kevin, "So much depended on the leaders. And now, since you have returned to strict Catholicism, and the leaders are not born again, or Baptized in the Spirit, how can you expect the Holy Spirit to keep those people going? The Charismatic Movement can only wither, where it is not permitted to be ecumenical."

14

A TRIP TO MEDJUGORJE

In June of 1981, the children of a family in the tiny Yugoslav village of Medjugorje began seeing a vision of the Virgin Mary. Each day, she would come to speak to them, and only the children themselves could see her. The local priest was convinced that the children were telling the truth, and pilgrims began to come and pray. In the process, many gave their lives to Christ, and told their friends, and full-scale revival has broken out. It is estimated that several hundred thousand Yugoslavs have had their lives changed and their faith renewed, as a result. As American Catholic Charismatics investigated, returned, and vouched for the authenticity of the vision, the author had to go and see for himself.

My introduction to the appearance of Mary in Yugoslavia was through the former Secretary of the Educational Department of the United Nations — an Austrian named Ernst Winters. I forget where we first

195

met, but we met again at a Pentecostal conference in
Europe, and as it often is with Christians, our friendship
had not faded in the interim. Then, some months later, I
am back in California, and I get a phone call from him.

"I'm in America, and I'm coming to California, and I
want to see you very, very much. Because I have
something extraordinary to share with you!"

So he came, and Anna had grown to like him; he was
an open and humble man. The first thing he said was: "I
have been to Yugoslavia to see an apparition of Mary." I
looked at him wide-eyed, as if I had seen an apparition
myself, but he just smiled and went on. "From my home,
it is only a day's drive. So I went, and I took my mother
with me. Privately, I was full of skepticism — what a
ridiculous thing! But curiosity outweighed doubt.

"When we got there, to my surprise there is Tom For-
rest, chairman of the Catholic Charismatic Central Committee in Rome. You know Tom," and I nodded. "Well,
all Tom said was, 'You ought to go into that vestry and
see what happens with this apparition talking to the
children.'

"It was happening every week, and sometimes more
often. I told Tom that I didn't know anybody, and how
was I to get in? He said that he would get me in. I asked
him about my mother, whom I couldn't very well leave
out, and he said for me to bring her, too. Then he explained to them that I was a special friend of his, highly
placed in the world, and it would be a great blessing, if
we could see this manifestation of God.

"So we went in, and saw the children praying, and all
of a sudden, my mother leaned over and whispered: 'I've
just seen Jesus. Jesus is here, and He just talked to me. He
said, "If you kneel, I will heal you." ' I looked around
and saw nothing, and then at my mother, who was badly

crippled with arthritis. Finally, I said, 'Mother, if Jesus is here, then there can be no mistake; this is His place. And if He said to kneel down, then you can do so, without falling.'

"She took a deep breath. 'All right,' she said, 'I'll try.' I could not see or hear whatever she did, but she managed to kneel down, and did not topple over. Instead, she raised her hands and said, 'I'm healed! Glory to God, I'm healed!' There was no pain, and I could see it was a miracle."

Ernst held out his hands, palms up. "After that, I had to believe that the apparition of Mary was real, even if I couldn't see it. Because Jesus would not have been there, otherwise. And after what my mother had seen and heard, and her miraculous deliverance from arthritis, there was no question that He was there."

Right then, I decided that I must go to see for myself. How did I feel about apparitions? Well, I had had no personal experience with them, but they were certainly Scriptural. The example I liked best was the one in the Book of Revelation (perhaps because I am nearing the end of my life, as the Apostle John was, on the isle of Patmos, when the angel came to him). Both times, John instinctively fell at the angel's feet in worship — only to be told to stop, for this was a fellow servant like himself and the other prophets, and like those who treasured the book he had written. Worship was for God alone . . . would this apparition of Mary be similar? Time would tell.

The pieces for my trip fell into place, and one of the key pieces was my friend, Dr. Peter Kuzmic, an Assembly of God pastor in Osijek, Yugoslavia, who had been with me in the World Council. I told him why I was coming and arranged to meet him in Zagreb, because I wanted to meet with the cardinal who had responsibility for Medjugorje.

When I arrived, Peter and I finally got to see Cardinal

Kuharic. "I remember you very well from the Vatican
Council," he said.

"You saw me there?"

"Yes, at the time I wasn't a cardinal, just an archbishop and I observed you, talking with the cardinals,
and so on. There is no doubt in my mind that God has
sent you here, because I was praying for Him to send
somebody with the right experience and deep spirituality,
to ask him to go and see this apparition and report on it.
Now," he smiled, "the Lord has sent you. And I didn't
even know you were coming."

"Well," I apologized, "I'm sorry; I didn't know your
address. I knew you were here, but I didn't know how to
get in touch with you."

Cardinal Kuharic smiled. "You see, it has worked out
beautifully." And he asked me to go to Medjugorje and
report back to him, as the next step was for him to apply to
the Holy Father in Rome, for authority to set up a formal
commission to study the phenomenon. He hoped to undo
the harm done, by the local bishop's resistance, and for
that he also needed John Paul's approval.

"But," I protested, "I want *your* evaluation."

The cardinal tapped his finger-tips. "How can I doubt
that this is God's doing? This apparition has been appearing for two years. They've just celebrated the second
anniversary, and police said that there were 140,000
people in front of that hill, where the first appearance
came, to children at a picnic. They have erected a huge
white cross on that mountain now, and do you know that
half a million young people have surrendered to Christ?
The Lord is stirring this country! They need fifty to sixty
priests every weekend, just to hear confessions and
to counsel these young people! And it's all because

this apparition tells them: "You are asking me questions that I cannot answer, because I don't know everything. Only Jesus, my Son, knows everything. Why don't you read the Bible, and see what He has to say? Because it is clear that you have no idea what He can do, and will do, for you and through you."

So, three of us — Peter Kuzmic, a Swedish missionary, and myself — left for Medjugorje. The first thing I noticed was that we literally did not see anyone who did not have a Bible under his arm. The first two fellows we spoke with (Peter acting as interpreter), were sitting under a tree, reading a Bible. Before we left them, I couldn't resist asking: "Have you been blessed by the phenomenon?"

"Oh yes, we have surrendered to Christ. Now we read what Jesus teaches."

"And who told you that?"

"The Mother says we must read the Bible."

Very quickly we ascertained that the whole revival was based on Scripture. Never in Yugoslavia had so many Bibles been distributed so swiftly. But there were problems. Mary was appearing to the children in a Franciscan Center, and the regional bishops did not like the Franciscans. So the local bishop put a priest in charge, with instructions to discourage and put a stop to the revival. But instead, the priest got converted! This so upset the bishop that he had the priest put in jail, telling the Communists that he was now encouraging the revival and had become politically dangerous. So they put the priest in jail, and he rejoiced, because it gave him more time to study the Scriptures.

I was tired, and we were fortunate to find a nice hotel, just a few miles from the church, which was out in the country. After a good nap and something to eat, we went

to the church. At 6:00 p.m., there was a celebration of the
eucharist, after which an hour was spent focussing on I
Corinthians 12, the gifts of the Spirit manifested. There
was tongues and interpretation, and prophecy, and all
manner of visions — it was wonderful! And I felt that the
Lord was there.

I wept and prayed, "Dear Lord, Your ways are
wonderful and mysterious. How can I explain these things
to other people? This is the kind of thing I have long
wanted to see, but I could never have suggested anything
like this, and here they are doing what I believe we ought to
do in our communion services. We ought to make
communion the central point and then go on to the
edification of the body through the gifts."

Afterwards, they invited us over to the monastery,
where they had lovely bread and plenty of grapes, which
were in season. Then they said to us, "Even if you had
gotten here early enough to attend the afternoon meeting,
you would not have seen any more than what we can show
you on videotape. The Mother has allowed us to tape one
session. And all you will hear is the girls having a
conversation with her, but you don't hear her voice, and,
of course, you don't see her at all." Now this puzzled me:
How can they say Mary is there, if nobody can see her, and
the tape did not capture her?

The next day, we went to visit the family. I wanted to
talk to the children, and the cardinal had said of the
oldest girl, who was 18, "That girl you must talk to. I
spent 2 hours with her, and she is a saint, fearless.
They've already threatened to kill her. But she told me that
the Mother said: 'Jesus is the Shepherd; He will not allow it
to happen.' And she's not afraid."

Her mother was with her, when we met, and when they
learned from Peter Kuzmic who I was and that I

loved Catholics and had been to the Vatican Council, and all the rest, they relaxed and began to confide in me. They seemed pleased that someone of my experience and background could understand what had happened to them.

So, through Peter, I asked her: "Tell me now, very slowly, how does it happen? You go there to pray, and the people around you go to pray."

"Yes," she said simply, "we just pray and praise God, and thank Him, and we feel rather expectant, naturally — 'Will she come this afternoon?' When suddenly our eyes open, and we can see her. When we see her, we don't see any other. The world is shut out. Next, she speaks, and we hear her . . . and then we begin to ask her questions — questions written out by people, you see. We read them to her, and write down what she says."

Sometimes, they didn't remember everything, but there was an amusing little fellow there, little Jacob, seven years old, and he remembered everything. There were just five children, all told, and they all saw her. I guess I sort of expected them to be different, somehow, perhaps ethereal. I have a real detestation of super-spiritual people, who insist on "waiting for the anointing" and then who shake and tremble when they pray for someone. That form of bragging upon their holiness I find extremely presumptuous.

But there was nothing of that sort here. These kids were as natural as they could be. They were sweet and humble; they could laugh, and they could weep, just like the happiest, healthiest kids I knew. And there was a doctor there, a medical man, who told me that what I had heard and what I had seen, was no different than what he had observed, and he had been with them for a long, long time; in fact, he had gotten converted through it all.

"As far as I am concerned, this is an absolutely genuine work of the Lord from the Holy Spirit."

Yet still, I intended to make up my own mind. And so, as we talked, I listened with all my senses. If there was anything — anything at all that was off anywhere — I wanted to be sure to pick it up. But if there was, the Lord shut my discernment to it. I heard nothing, saw nothing, felt nothing, that would in any way put me off. And now they began to talk about the sort of thing that Mary would tell them. They said that she had repeatedly warned them that she, and her prayers, could not accomplish any more than they and their prayers. "I have no privilege," she told them, "I am not preferred above anybody. I am just like you are, and you have the privilege to talk to Jesus personally without me." And that was why they then went out and knelt down before the priest and talked to Jesus.

When I heard that, I no longer had any doubt about the authenticity and validity of the apparition. Those children would never say that they got saved through Mary; she sent them to Jesus every time. Now I knew what Fr. John Bertolucci had meant, when he told me: "David, this is a charismatic Mary!"

Yes, she was, and you could imagine our conversation in the car, as the three of us drove away from Medjugorje, and headed for the city of Osijek where Peter's church was, and where we would go to meeting tomorrow, it being Sunday. I was glad that we had gone through proper channels, and seen the cardinal first, and would be reporting back to him, while so many others had just gone straight to Medjugorje and gone off to write their articles and things. And I was confident that my report would be useful to him, in his application to Rome, for authority to establish a commission.

But in the meantime, God had something else in store for me. We had reached the outskirts of Osijek and found a nice hotel, when Peter confided to me: "Brother David, you may be the only man that can help us to change a bad situation. Here, in this area of Yugoslavia, I am considered the leading pastor. I've got one of the oldest churches, since when I came there, they had just been able to get the old Jewish synagogue from the government, which was standing empty, and they gave it to us. And when they heard that I had a doctorate from a Catholic university and so on, and wanted to open a college, the government granted me permission to raise money and build a three-story academic building." He paused, not knowing quite how to say the next. "But — I am pastor of a church that is supposed to be Pentecostal, and they tell me that nobody has received the Baptism in the congregation in 20 years. Twenty years! And if I go over an hour in a meeting, brother, are the brakes on; I mean, they just get up and walk out!" He stared at the floor, shaking his head as he spoke. "It is a dead, dead, dead, miserable, old church." And then he looked up at me. "Can we — change it?"

"Well," I said, "that depends on what the Lord wants to do. When a Pentecostal church goes dead, there is nothing deader! But while you were talking, I was already thinking that tomorrow morning I would tell them about what Jesus is doing in the world, and what's happening in the churches, and I'll make Jesus very real to them. Then we'll encourage them to come back in the evening, and I'll confront them with Jesus the Baptizer, and we'll see what happens."

Peter was excited then; we both were. And so, with Peter acting as my interpreter, we had a wonderful morning meeting. I told them about the visit to Med-jugorje, which we had just come from, and also about what was happening in Rome and America and all over the place. I got excited, just telling them about it!

After we had said goodbye to them, Peter exclaimed with a grin, "You have really persuaded these people! I'm sure tonight that this big old church will be full!"

And it was. On the platform with us were the two old men who had pastored that church before Peter. They were on their way to a Pentecostal pastors' conference in Vienna the next day, to which Peter had also been invited, and curiosity had brought them here.

Right from the beginning of the meeting, I made it very plain to all present how I felt about the Baptism in the Holy Spirit. "If Jesus Christ Himself could not minister without this Baptism," I put it to them, "how dare you, any of you in this place, think that you could do anything that Jesus wants you to do, without this anointing, without this Baptism?" I looked around the church, at one and then another, to see if anyone would respond. "All right, then, tonight be baptized! Men *and* women! I challenge you to come and ask Jesus to baptize you. I will not lay hands on you. I want to have nothing to do with it, anymore than to just tell you. You come up here and sit in the first pew. On the Day of Pentecost, they were sitting, and so you don't need to take any other position."

Immediately, a long-haired young fellow came forward and turned and spoke to the congregation: "You know the Lord saved me, and now I'm ready for this blessing. I need it!"

Peter whispered to me, "That was one of the worst drug-addicted hippies in this city." The young fellow sat in the end of the front row, and the rest of the pew quickly filled up. I called for the ushers to ask the people to open up the next pew, and then said, "Jesus makes no distinction between men and women; He'll baptize the latter just like the former." At that, a few ladies came forward and sat down at the end of the open pew. I went on: "On the Day of Pentecost, Mary herself received the Baptism. And if Mary needed the Baptism, none of you — " I paused, then recalled what I had once said to some Catholic sisters in France, at the first reconciliation meeting I had convened between the Catholics and the Huguenots. "You may be Mother Superior, but you can never be superior to Mary; you need the Baptism."

Now many ladies came forward. And afterwards, one who was elegantly dressed and of upright bearing, came to me and said: "Do you know me?"

"No," I smiled, "I'm afraid I don't know anyone here."

"But you pointed right at me, when you said, 'You may be Mother Superior, but you can't be superior to Mary.' "

"Are you a Mother Superior?" I asked, and she nodded. "But how could I have known? You don't have a habit on."

"Yes, but before I left my room tonight I said, 'Lord, tonight you must tell me very clearly, very simply, whether I need this Baptism,' and then you pointed directly at me."

I laughed. "That's what we call the word of knowledge."

She did receive the Baptism that night, and I chuckled to think what would now happen in that convent.

Next to be touched were the two old men on the platform. What they were witnessing had never happened while they had been there — perhaps it should have. Among those who came forward was one of the two old

men, who had been bitter, bitter enemies of the former
pastors and had driven them to resign. This man's wife had
received the Baptism, and he had forbidden her ever to pray
in tongues in his presence. Now, here he came, and you
could hear a ripple run through the congregation. "You
sit down," I said, pointing to the front pew, and he did.

Then, to everyone's surprise, his wife came forward
and stood in front of him and began to pray in tongues.
He got up, grabbed her — and started praying in tongues
himself! When that happened, the two former pastors
started weeping, and knowing they understood English, I
turned around and said, "I cannot speak your language,
so there's no use me going, but will you go down and help
the people? Go on, there are people you need to talk to."

Like a shot, one of them went to the far back of the
congregation and embraced his enemy and brought him
forward, and he, too, got the Baptism. All told, twenty
people were baptized in the Spirit that night, and instead
of leaving after an hour, or an hour and a half, they
stayed four hours. For we had wave upon wave of glory,
and no one wanted to go home or take a chance of miss-
ing anything. Peter was overjoyed. "That which was
dead is now alive!"

When we got to his home late that night, and he told
his wife, who was home nursing children with whooping
cough, what had happened, she joined our rejoicing.
"Now you must go to Vienna," she declared, "and take
David with you. For God has used him to raise a dead
Pentecostal church, and that's a miracle!"

So we went, and arrived late enough, so that when we
finally found a pensione with two unoccupied rooms, I
went straight to bed. But Peter set out to find the conference, and see if anything was still going on. When he

did, they asked him: "What did you bring du Plessis for? He's not Pentecostal."

That angered Peter, who said, "If he's not Pentecostal, how in the world could twenty people in my church receive the Baptism last night, under his ministry? And if David du Plessis hadn't preached, I don't think anyone would have received the Baptism."

"You mean, he still encourages this?"

"Why," Peter declared, "he's better than anybody else I've ever heard."

They were doubly surprised, because they had also heard that Peter Kuzmic was no longer Pentecostal, either. So they invited him, then and there, to speak, and he told them the happy news of his re-awakened church, and of my role in the resurrection. They were dumbfounded! The next morning, when I came to the meeting, I sat to one side, so as not to disturb anyone, and afterwards young pastors came up and welcomed me and told me how their fathers had known me.

After that conference, the Pentecostal attitude throughout Europe changed towards me — and all because of a trip to Medjugorje.

I have a file in which I keep all the latest information on Medjugorje, for I am looking forward to seeing what the final chapter will be. Do I think there will be other such phenomena? I certainly do! According to the New Testament, they were not that uncommon at the beginning of this age; angels even appeared to the believers. And now that we are coming to the end of this age, it makes sense that such things should occur again. When I was a young man, I saw my share of visions, and now as an old man, I am enjoying some heaven-sent dreams. And who knows? Before I die, I might even see an angel or two.